Business Cards
The Art of Saying Hello

D1808257

LAURENCE KING PUBLISHING
in association with
HARPER DESIGN INTERNATIONAL
an imprint of HarperCollins*Publishers*

LAURENCE KING

Published in 2004
by Laurence King Publishing Ltd
71 Great Russell Street
London WC1B 3BP
United Kingdom
Tel_ +44 20 7430 8850
Fax_ +44 20 7430 8880
E_ enquiries@laurenceking.co.uk
www.laurenceking.co.uk

First published in the United States
in 2004 by
Harper Design International
An imprint of
HarperCollins*Publishers*
10 East 53rd Street
New York, NY 10022
Fax: (212) 207 7654

Harper Collins books may be
purchased for educational,
business, or sales promotional use.
For information, please write to:
Special Markets Department,
HarperCollins*Publishers* Inc., 10
East 53rd Street, New York, NY
10022.

A catalogue record for this book is
available from the British Library.

Library of Congress Control
Number: 2004106493

ISBN 1 85669 386 4

Printed in China
First Printing, 2004

Words
Liz Farrelly

Design
Michael Dorrian

Selected by
Michael Dorrian
Liz Farrelly

Thanks to
Jorge Alderete_ Rilla Alexander_
Sean Alexander_ Phil Ashcroft_
Rik Bas Backer_ Gilles Bachmann_
Charlie Banks_ Jon Barlow_ Paula
Benson_ Gary Benzel_ Anna Bird_
Lineke van den Boezem_ Helen
Bottomley_ Sarah Bruce_ Boris
Brumnjak_ Stefan Bucher_ Richard
Bull_ Mike Carney_ David Carson_
Martin Carty_ Toko Chan_ Martin
Cox_ Adam Cruickshank_ David
Zack Custer_ Frédérique Daubal_
Andy Day_ Dave Denis_ Andrew
Diprose_ Miles Donovan_ Andrea
Dreier_ James-Lee Duffy_ Taylor
Deupree_ Alan Dye_ Bryan
Edmondson_ Kira Elise_ Glenna
Ellen_ Brendan Elliott_ Tim Everist_
Marc Fiebelkorn_ Fishburn-Hedges_
Kevin Foulkes_ Donna Fullman_
Sarah Gaventa_ Dave Gibson_
Nicky Gibson_ Sabine Gilhuijs_
Paul Wesley Griggs_ Peter Grundy_
Nevs Hamling_ Todd Hansson_
Tim Head_ Joost van der Heijden_
Sally Hems_ Richard Hennings_
Amanda Hopewell_ Nat Hunter_
Chris Hutchinson_ Carl Ison_ Keiji
Ito_ Karen Jane_ Tim Jester_ Todd
St.John_ Jeroen Jongeleen_ Jens
Kajus_ Marc Kappeler_ Alan
Kavanagh_ René Etienne Keller_
Frith Kerr_ Billy Kiossoglou_ Fanny
Khoo_ Joost Korngold_ Joe Kral_
Henrik Kubel_ Christian Küsters_

Nathan Lauder_ Pit Lederle_
Josh Van Lemmeren_ Michael
Lenz_ Joe Lucchese_ Birte Ludwig_
Linda Lundin_ Anja Lutz_ Matthew
McCarthy_ Andrew McGovern_
Chris Merrick_ Craig Metzger_ Paul
Miller_ Patrick Monnier_ Julian
Morey_ Fraser Muggeridge_ Sean
Murphy_ Mysterious Al_ Nina
Nägel_ Kurosh Nasseri_ Amelia
Noble_ Toke Nygaard_ Hanni
Pannier_ Ben Parker_ Scott Parker_
Simon Parkes_ Matt Pattinson_
Axel Pfaender_ Frank Philippin_
Monica Pirovano_ Seb Pizzutto_
Michael C Place_ Roy Poh_
Andrew Rae_ Alexandra Ramildi_
Hazel Rattigan_ David Recchia_
Abby Ribband_ Paul Rickus_ Kerry
Roper_ Anja Rosendahl_ Gerard
Saint_ Mikey Seiler_ Segura Inc_
Stephen Sorrell_ Peter Spreenberg_
Start Creative_ Peter Stemmler_
Martin Stillhart_ Phil Stuart_ Ian
Styles_ Patrick Sundqvist_ Akira
Takahashi_ So Takahashi_ Roger
Fawcett-Tang_ Kate Thomas_
Patrick Thomas_ Mark Thomson_
Ben Tibbs_ Jake Tilson_ Yorgo
Tloupas_ Clarissa Tossin_ Barbara
Valicenti_ Marc-A Valli_ Gregg
Virostek_ Jan Voss_ Tim Watson_
Simon Waterfall_ Josh Welsher_
Sam Wiehl_ Sam Winston_ Paul
Winter_ Martin Woodtli_ Woody_

There are two sides to every business card. OK, anomalies do exist: some cards have multiple personalities; others are soothingly holistic…and we'll deal with those later. But generally, with the two-sided variety, there's the side with something fancy on it and the side with the info, the guts.

For some people, though, that's going too far; they prefer one-sided cards that fit inside plastic wallets inside folders, so you can flip through without the inconvenience of having to get the thing out. That's a little too regimented for me, as apart from the sides, there's the edges, the texture and the smell of cards to enjoy. Plus, they look nice propped around a desk, pinned to the wall or, if they're 3-D, stuck on top of your Mac.

Getting back to the duality of cards. What most cards do is tell a stranger something about you. On the one hand, something very conscious and concrete, about your physical place in the world; and on the other, something subconscious and less easily defined…about your personality. Unless of course you work for a massive corporation, and everyone from the CEO to the most junior salesperson has the same card. (This is to be avoided.)

There are choices to make from the word go, about the information you want to impart. You may give only your mobile number, i.e. you're a nomad; or you might position yourself entirely digitally, in the ether, via a web address. Then there's how you define yourself; whether via a job title or a self-imposed epithet. With new ways of working (at home, on the road) and with many more people multi-tasking, these days cards have a lot more to say. Whatever information you

offer, bear in mind that it will be read, no matter how easy or difficult you, or your designer, makes that task.

When we start to consider the design of a card, other choices you make will give a whole lot away about your personality. How orderly are you? Do you keep your cards in a mini folder so the edges don't crease? That will dictate the dimensions. Are you strapped for cash and hate to spend money on printer's bills, so you make your own cards from scraps and scrawls? Are you so achingly spontaneous that you need a new card every day, firing up the Mac before you leave for that important meeting? Are you glamorous, traditional, inventive, austere, colourful, still playing with toys, ostentatious, functional? And, if you're a designer, this is the one you want them to ask: are you creative?

This book is a collection of business cards, a very personal selection by Michael Dorrian and myself. Michael started it with his obsessive collecting, asking everyone he met for their card. He'd rifle through my desk looking for new ones I'd accumulated. Some I'd keep to myself though...

Making no excuses for our tastes in graphic design and visual statements, this book isn't a comprehensive one-of-every-kind collection; it isn't a didactic "how to" manual either. There are no chapters; instead the contents are arranged into overlapping sections according to a card's aesthetic: so typography turns into illustration, into photography, into special materials, then assemblages and do-it-yourself.

Michael and I think this selection of cards is inspirational. How did we choose them? We put out the word to contacts far and wide, as well as following up on cards in our collection. The "wow" factor was the final decider. Did a card make us stop in our tracks and say, "look at that!"? They did, for many different reasons.

The only problem now is that you might want to take a second look at your own card. If you want to contact any of the people in this book, their details are included!

Start Creative Limited
2 Sheraton Street
Soho
London W1F 8BH

Michael Dorrian
Senior Designer

tel +44 (0)20 7269 0101
fax +44 (0)20 7269 0102
web www.startcreative.co.uk

dl +44 (0)20 7269 0148
em michael@startcreative.co.uk

Anarchy is order

Design
  Start Creative

For
  Start Creative_
  Creative agency_
  London, UK

Info
Each item of stationery has a different, symbolic found letter
on its reverse, which together spell Start. The card's "A" relates
to destruction as a creative act. The restrained typography of
the flip-side hints at Start's dual personality.

Paul Austin...
Tel +44 (0)20 7490 4006
Mobile 07968 057 410
Fax +44 (0)20 7490 2991
Email paul@madethought.co...
www.madethought.com

MadeThought.

Second Floor,
81 Cannon Street Road, London E...
UK

<table>
<tr><td><u>Design</u></td><td><u>For</u></td><td><u>Info</u></td></tr>
<tr><td>Made Thought</td><td>Made Thought_</td><td>Bright, sharp and informative, Made Thought's no-nonsense</td></tr>
<tr><td>Paul Austin_</td><td>Designers_</td><td>typography is given a touch of glamour with silver-foil blocking</td></tr>
<tr><td>Ben Parker</td><td>London, UK</td><td>on uncoated stock.</td></tr>
</table>

The Designers Republic. Generic.

The Workstation 15 Paternoster Row Sheffield S1 2BX United Kingdom.
E: dr@thedesignersrepublic.com
URL: www.thedesignersrepublic.com
P: +44 [0] 114 275 4982.
F: +44 [0] 114 275 9127.
ISDN: +44 [0] 114 276 6339.

TDR is a division of Pho-Ku Corp.
1-6 3F Daikanyama-cho Shibuya-ku
Tokyo 150-0034 Japan.
〒150-0034 東京都渋谷区代官山町 1-6 3F
F: +81 3 3496 0747

THE DESIGNERS REPUBLIC LTD
THE WORKSTATION 15 PATERNOSTER ROW, SHEFFIELD S1 2BX
[53°23'N 01°28'W] SOYO. UNITED KINGDOM.
E: DR@THEDESIGNERSREPUBLIC.COM
URL S: WWW.THEDESIGNERSREPUBLIC.COM/
WWW.PHO-KU.COM/ WWW.PHO-KU-BUREAU.COM/ WWW.PHO-KU.COM
PH: +44 [0] 114 275 4982. FACS: +44 [0] 114 275 9127
ISDN: +44 [0] 114 276 6339

TO BE GIVEN
UP ON REQUEST

The Workstation 15 Paternoster Row Sheffield S1 2BX United Kingdom.
E: dr@thedesignersrepublic.com
URL: www.thedesignersrepublic.com
P: +44 [0] 114 275 4982.
F: +44 [0] 114 275 9127.
ISDN: +44 [0] 114 276 6339.

TDR is a division of Pho-Ku Corp.
1-6 3F Daikanyama-cho Shibuya-ku
Tokyo 150-0034 Japan.
〒150-0034 東京都渋谷区代官山町 1-6 3F
F: +81 3 3496 0747

Administration.

The Workstation 15 Paternoster Row Sheffield S1 2BX United Kingdom.
E: shelley@thedesignersrepublic.com
URL: www.thedesignersrepublic.com
P: +44 [0] 114 275 4982.
F: +44 [0] 114 275 9127.
ISDN: +44 [0] 114 276 6339.

TDR is a division of Pho-Ku Corp.
1-6 3F Daikanyama-cho Shibuya-ku
Tokyo 150-0034 Japan.
〒150-0034 東京都渋谷区代官山町 1-6 3F
F: +81 3 3496 0747

THE DESIGNERS REPUBLIC LTD
THE WORKSTATION 15 PATERNOSTER ROW, SHEFFIELD S1 2BX
[53°23'N 01°28'W] SOYO. UNITED KINGDOM.
E: ABBY@THEDESIGNERSREPUBLIC.COM
URL S: WWW.THEDESIGNERSREPUBLIC.COM/
WWW.PHO-KU.COM/ WWW.PHO-KU-BUREAU.COM/ WWW.PHO-KU.COM
PH: +44 [0] 114 275 4982. FACS: +44 [0] 114 275 9127
ISDN: +44 [0] 114 276 6339

TO BE GIVEN
UP ON REQUEST

The Workstation 15 Paternoster Row Sheffield S1 2BX United Kingdom.
E: abby@thedesignersrepublic.com
URL: www.thedesignersrepublic.com
P: +44 [0] 114 275 4982.
F: +44 [0] 114 275 9127.
ISDN: +44 [0] 114 276 6339.

TDR is a division of Pho-Ku Corp.
1-6 3F Daikanyama-cho Shibuya-ku
Tokyo 150-0034 Japan.
〒150-0034 東京都渋谷区代官山町 1-6 3F
F: +81 3 3496 0747

The Workstation 15 Paternoster Row Sheffield S1 2BX United Kingdom.

The Workstation 15 Paternoster Row Sheffield S1 2BX United Kingdom.

The Workstation 15 Paternoster Row Sheffield S1 2BX United Kingdom.
E:dave@thedesignersrepublic.com
URL:www.thedesignersrepublic.com
P:+44[0]114 275 4982.
F:+44[0]114 275 9127.
ISDN:+44[0]114 276 6339.

TDR is a division of Pho-Ku Corp.
1-6 3F Daikanyama-cho Shibuya-ku
Tokyo 150-0034 Japan.
〒150-0034 東京都渋谷区代官山町 1-6 3F
F:+81 3 3496 0747

The Workstation 15 Paternoster Row Sheffield S1 2BX United Kingdom.
E:matt@thedesignersrepublic.com
URL:www.thedesignersrepublic.com
P:+44[0]114 275 4982.
F:+44[0]114 275 9127.
ISDN:+44[0]114 276 6339.

TDR is a division of Pho-Ku Corp.
1-6 3F Daikanyama-cho Shibuya-ku
Tokyo 150-0034 Japan.
〒150-0034 東京都渋谷区代官山町 1-6 3F
F:+81 3 3496 0747

The Workstation 15 Paternoster Row Sheffield S1 2BX United Kingdom.
E:nick@thedesignersrepublic.com
URL:www.thedesignersrepublic.com
P:+44[0]114 275 4982.
M:+44[0]7775 681 807.
F:+44[0]114 275 9127.

TDR is a division of Pho-Ku Corp.
1-6 3F Daikanyama-cho Shibuya-ku
Tokyo 150-0034 Japan.
〒150-0034 東京都渋谷区代官山町 1-6 3F
F:+81 3 3496 0747

The Workstation 15 Paternoster Row Sheffield S1 2BX United Kingdom.
E:mike@thedesignersrepublic.com
URL:www.thedesignersrepublic.com
P:+44[0]114 275 4982.
M:+44[0]7977 457 407.
F:+44[0]114 275 9127.

TDR is a division of Pho-Ku Corp.
1-6 3F Daikanyama-cho Shibuya-ku
Tokyo 150-0034 Japan.
〒150-0034 東京都渋谷区代官山町 1-6 3F
F:+81 3 3496 0747

Design
The Designers
Republic

For
The Designers
Republic_
Designers_
Sheffield, UK

Info
Subtle variations within a vivid colour palette married to
information-heavy text add up to The Designers Republic
aesthetic in miniature.

sierra/tango/romeo/
uniform/kilo/tango/
uniform/romeo_
delta/echo/sierra/
india/golf/november

telephone:
plus four/four (zero)
one/four/nine/three_
seven/zero/one/
seven/six/six

see air rah/tang
go/row me oh/
you nee form/key loh/
tang go/you nee
form/row me oh

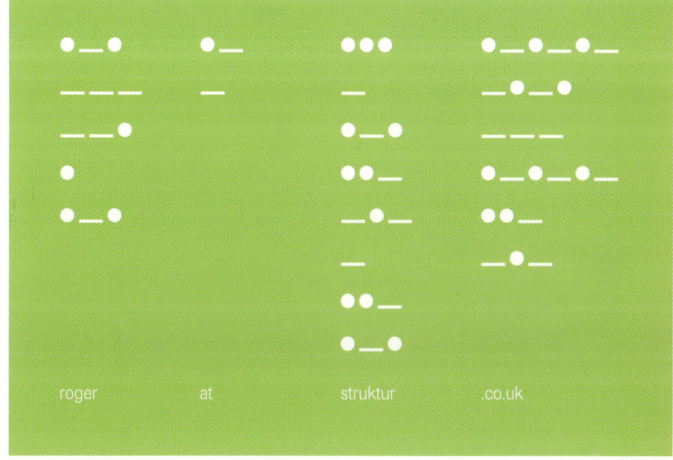

roger   at   struktur   .co.uk

Design
Struktur Design
Roger Fawcett-Tang

For
Struktur Design_
Designers_
London, UK

Info
The company name is spelt out using the international "radio
speak" code, while the phone number is rendered in words.
A second version progresses to phonetic spelling and morse
code, illustrating that there is a point at which too much
information may complicate matters.

EYEFI.INTERACTIVE.◖◗**.**
DIGITAL ARCHITECTS.THE NETHERLANDS.
W.G.PLEIN.369-373.1054SG.AMSTERDAM.
[ᵀᴱᴸ]+31(0)20,3207440.[ᶠᴬˣ]+31(0)20,3207442.[ᵁᴿᴸ]WWW.EYEFI.NL
PAUL.RICKUS.
ART DIRECTOR.
PAULRICKUS@EYEFI.NL

EYEFI.INTERACTIVE.◖◗. W.G. PLEIN 369-373. 1054SG. AMSTERDAM. TEL.+31(0)20,3207440.

Design
 Eyefi.interactive
 Paul Rickus

For
 Eyefi.interactive_
 Digital architects_
 Amsterdam,
 The Netherlands

Info
 Printed in a satiny spot varnish, the density of information
 on these cards is rendered decorative, almost ethereal.

ooooo**evolve**DEVELOPMENT

Ashley Williams

10 Wellington Street St.Kilda 3182 Victoria
T 61 3 9526 5180
F 61 3 9526 5112
M 0407 315 481
E awilliams@evolvedevelopment.com.au

ACN 104 808 979

Design
 Clear
 Matthew McCarthy
Typography
 Andrew Trevillian

For
 Evolve
 Development_
 Property developers_
 Melbourne,
 Australia

Info
Reflecting a subtle use of materials and form, the marque for this
development company changes from a circle to a square, via
vector-based shapes and a gradual tonal shift.

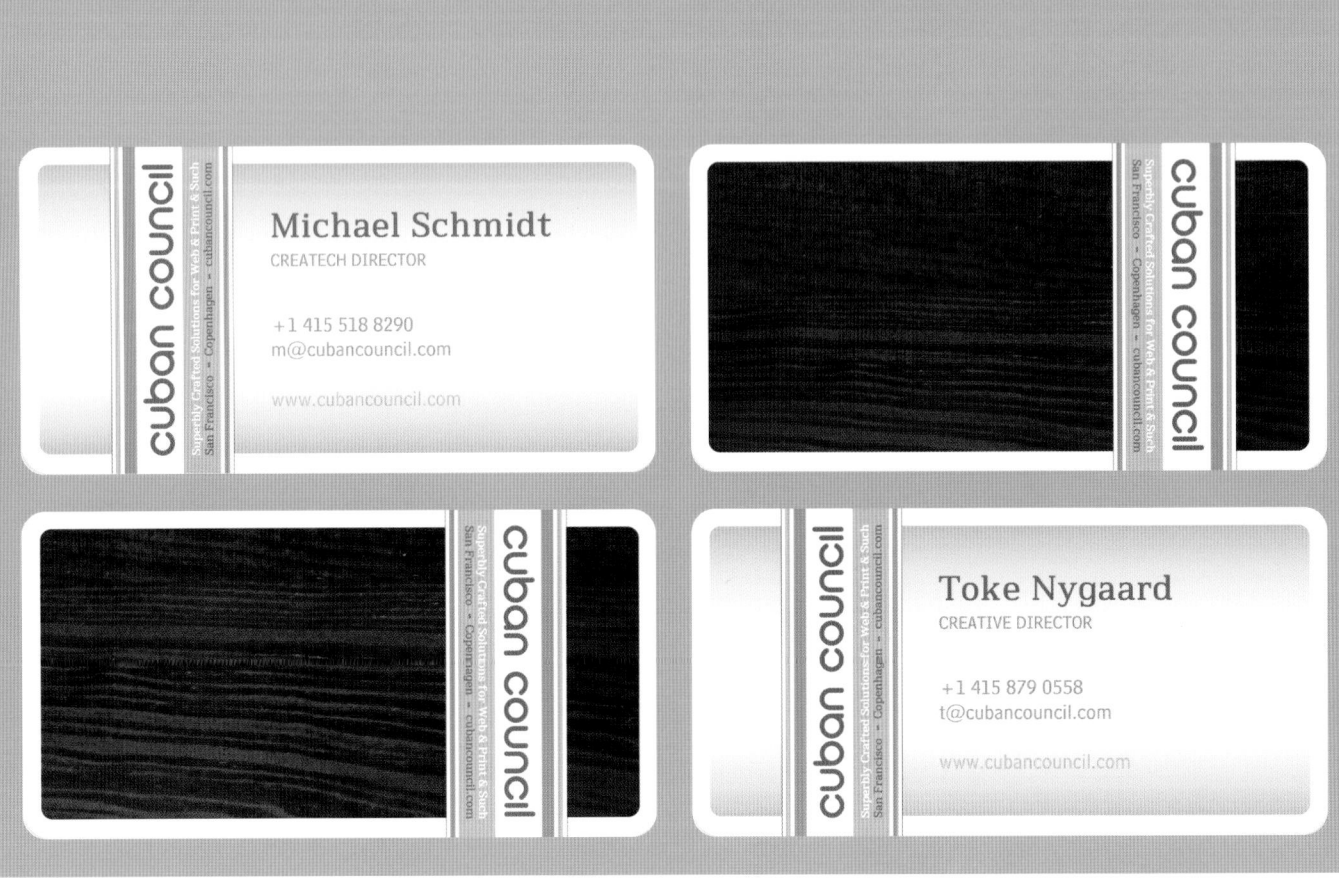

Design
Cuban Council

For
Cuban Council
Designers_
Copenhagen,
Denmark

Info
The kitsch graphic language of cigar boxes is used
to create a nostalgic, heavily-themed card.

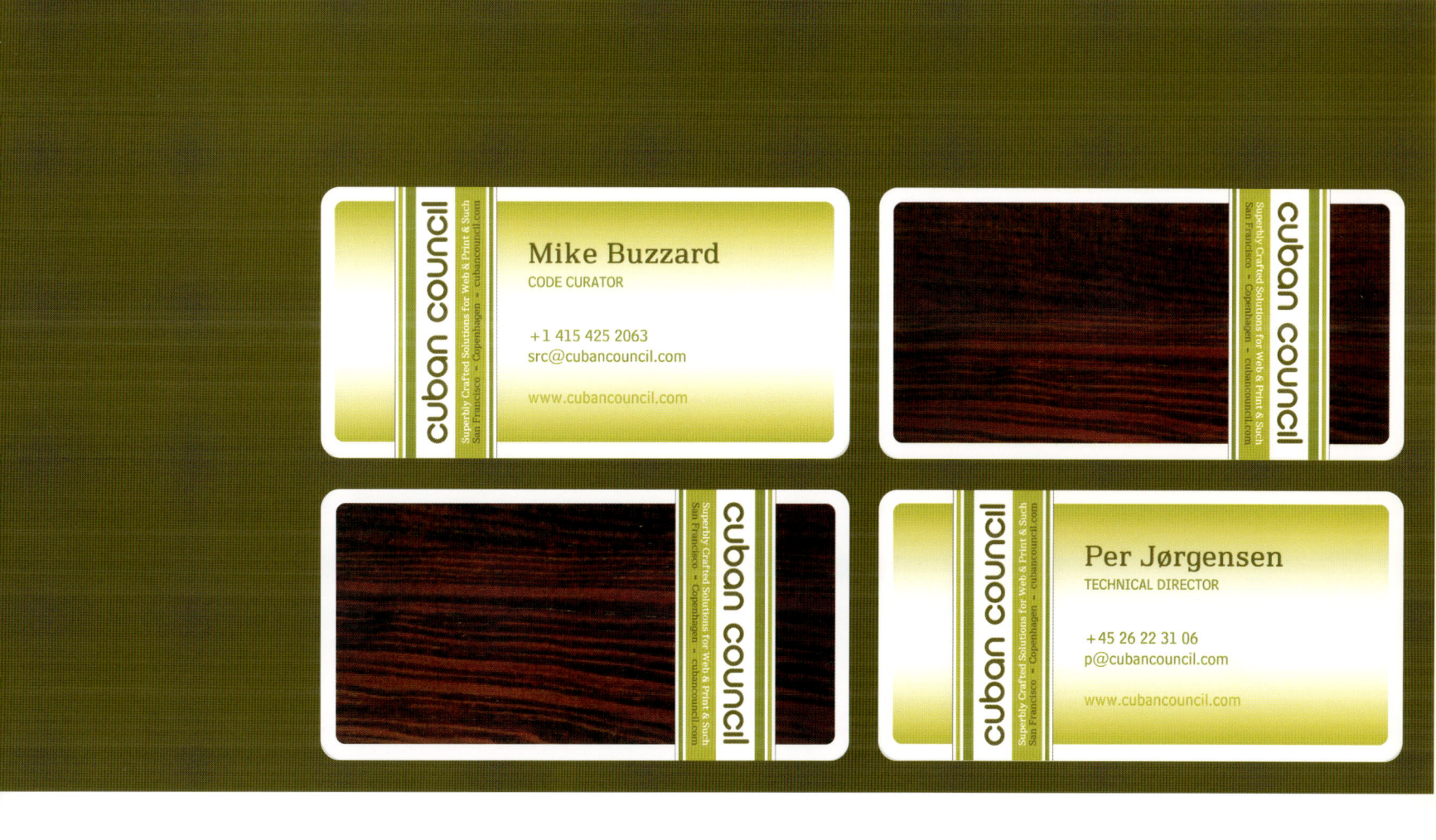

cuban council

Superbly Crafted Solutions for Web & Print & Such
San Francisco ~ Copenhagen ~ cubancouncil.com

Mike Buzzard

CODE CURATOR

+1 415 425 2063
src@cubancouncil.com

www.cubancouncil.com

cuban council

Superbly Crafted Solutions for Web & Print & Such
San Francisco ~ Copenhagen ~ cubancouncil.com

cuban council

Superbly Crafted Solutions for Web & Print & Such
San Francisco ~ Copenhagen ~ cubancouncil.com

cuban council

Superbly Crafted Solutions for Web & Print & Such
San Francisco ~ Copenhagen ~ cubancouncil.com

Per Jørgensen

TECHNICAL DIRECTOR

+45 26 22 31 06
p@cubancouncil.com

www.cubancouncil.com

Design
  BCDesign

For
  BCDesign
  Designers_
  Seattle, USA

Info
A hierarchy of information and pattern is established by
printing on both sides of translucent plastic; it's shaped to
approximate a futuristic "boarding card".

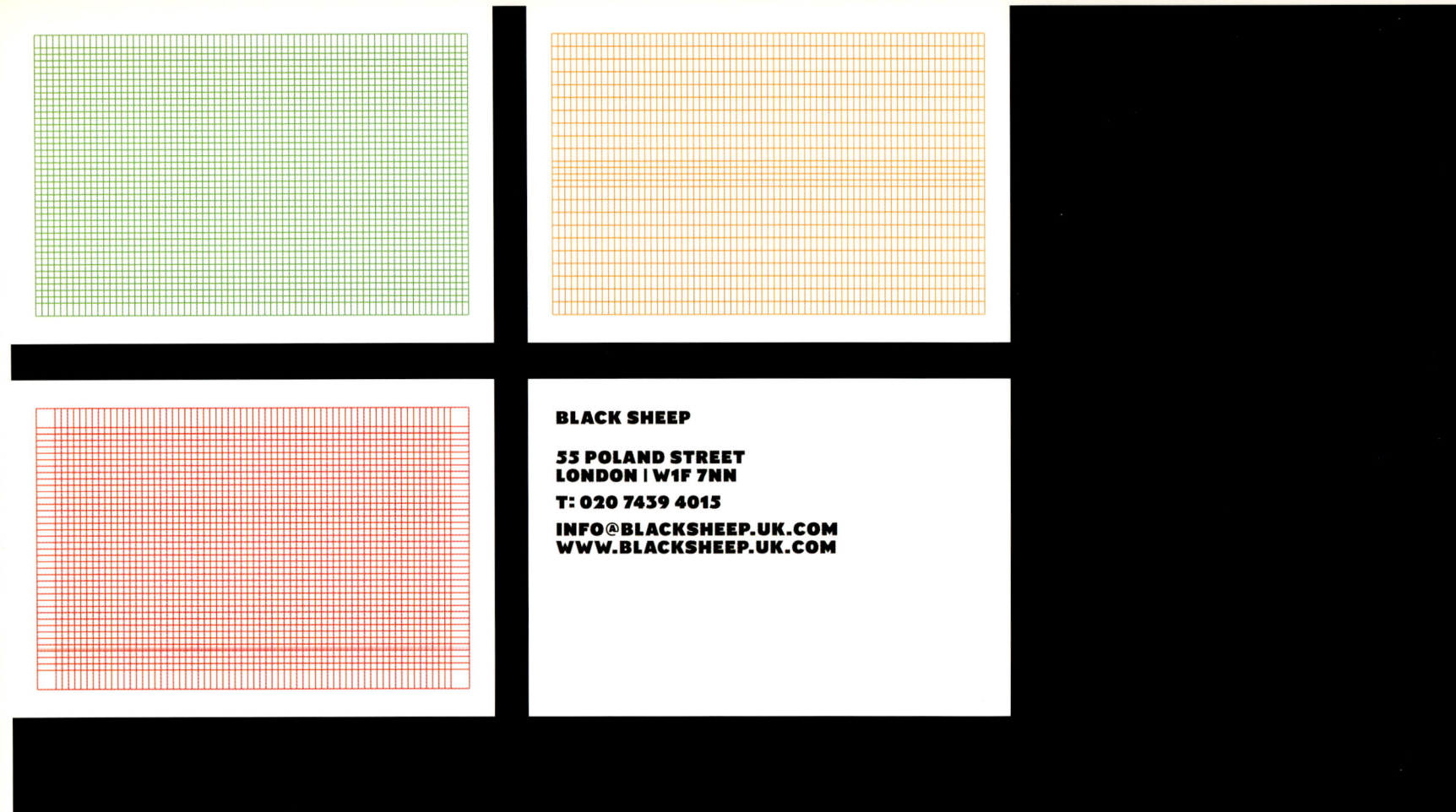

BLACK SHEEP

55 POLAND STREET
LONDON | W1F 7NN

T: 020 7439 4015

INFO@BLACKSHEEP.UK.COM
WWW.BLACKSHEEP.UK.COM

<u>Design</u>
Kerr Noble

<u>For</u>
Black Sheep
Recruitment_
agency_
London, UK

<u>Info</u>
A series of grids for each element of this recruitment agency's
stationery reflects their aim of placing the right candidate in the
right position; a job-finding maze becomes the company structure.

Design
Martin Woodtli

For
Martin Woodtli_
Designer_
Zurich, Switzerland

Info
For passing telephone numbers around. Simply mark your
number on the keypad-style matrix and hand it over.

Big-Active	Fuck off
Big-Active Limited	Big-Active Limited
Hello	Card
Big-Active Limited	Big-Active Limited

Design
Big Active
Paul Hetherington_
Gerard Saint_
Mark Watkins

For
Big Active_
Designers_
London, UK

Info
Inspired by "learn to read" cards, the set included one phrase meant for door-to-door salesmen who unfailingly ask for a card while being escorted from the premises.

<u>Design</u>
pre>loaded

<u>For</u>
pre>loaded_
Designers_
London, UK

<u>Info</u>
Taking their inspiration from everyday life, pre>loaded chose blue for their cards, as inspired by the name of their local pub; the rounded corners signify the "bulge" of lager at the top of a glass; the anagrams are attempts to spell the company name after a night's drinking.

Peter Chadwick
Art Director
ZiP Design
07970 004 670
peter@zipdesign.co.uk

Unit 2A Queens Studio
121 Salusbury Road London NW6 6RG
T 020 7372 4474 F 020 7372 4484
ISDN 020 7328 2816
www.zipdesign.co.uk

Charlie Banks
Studio & Account Co-ordinator
ZiP Design
07970 004 674
charlie@zipdesign.co.uk

Unit 2A Queens Studio
121 Salusbury Road London NW6 6RG
T 020 7372 4474 F 020 7372 4484
ISDN 020 7328 2816
www.zipdesign.co.uk

Design
Zip Design
Peter Chadwick

Client
Zip Design_
Designers_
London, UK

Info
This boy–girl partnership render their logo in playful baby
blue and pink so as to differentiate their cards.

three forty four design
Stefan G. Bucher

101 n.grand avenue, suite 7
telephone: 626.796.5148

pasadena, ca 91103.3576
e-mail: stefan@344design.com

Design
 344 Design
 Stefan G Bucher

For
 344 Design_
 Designers_
 Pasadena,
 USA

Info
 Stefan uses the glittery stickers as "teaser" cards, handing them
 to people who immediately ask for more information. They then
 have a habit of sticking around.

POKE
NICKY
NICKY@POKELONDON.COM

NICKY GIBSON
POKE
THE TEA BUILDING
REDCHURCH STREET
LONDON E2 7DJ

+44 (0)207 3245 128

POKE
IAIN
IAIN@POKELONDON.COM

POKE
SIMON
SIMON@POKELONDON.COM

POKE
NICK
NICK@POKELONDON.COM

POKE
SIMONK
SIMONK@POKELONDON.COM

POKE
PETER
PETER@POKELONDON.COM

POKE
TOM
TOM@POKELONDON.COM

POKE
NICOLAS
NIK@POKELONDON.COM

Design
Poke
Nicky Gibson

For
Poke_
New media
designers_
London, UK

Info
Each staffer is colour coded; bold typography
turns the company name into a command.

28

伊藤桂司
Keiji ITO

〒154-0016
東京都世田谷区弦巻5-6-16
弦巻リハイム903
有限会社ユー・エフ・ジー

#903 Tsurumaki REHEIM 5-6-16
Tsurumaki Setagaya-ku Tokyo
154-0016
Phone:03-3420-8471
Fax:03-3420-8472
Mobile:090-9383-0326
E-mail:ron@t3.rim.or.jp
URL:http://www.site-ufg.com

秋山曜子
Yoco AKIYAMA

〒154-0016
東京都世田谷区弦巻5-6-16
弦巻リハイム903
有限会社ユー・エフ・ジー

#903 Tsurumaki REHEIM 5-6-16
Tsurumaki Setagaya-ku Tokyo
154-0016
Phone:03-3420-8471
Fax:03-3420-8472
Mobile:090-9674-2606
E-mail:akiyama@ft.catv.ne.jp
URL:http://www.y-pulse.com

Design
UFG Inc
Yoco Akiyama

For
UFG Inc_
Designers_
Tokyo, Japan

Info
Strong typography and the repetitious use of the company's
logo are enlivened via subtle colour variations.

Design
Build
Michael C Place

For
Inferno Games_
Games designers_
New York, USA

Info
With levels of information tailored to various needs, a decoding
legend, cheeky hidden messages and go-faster stripes, these
sheets of cards may be folded, torn or framed.

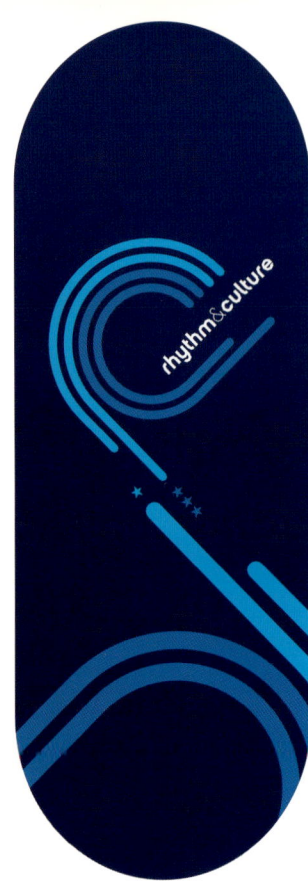

Design
Mesh
Paul Miller_
Akira Takahashi

For
Rhythm & Culture_
Music store_
Washington DC,
USA

Info
A memorable card thanks to its unique shape and the
marriage of subtly-coloured abstract devices and text.

32

Design
Mesh
Paul Miller_
Akira Takahashi

For
Kurosh Nasseri_
Music consultant_
Washington DC,
USA

Info
A logo extrapolated into an intricate surface pattern, which cleverly accommodates the contact details, to create an out of the ordinary card for a lawyer, albeit one working in the image-conscious music industry.

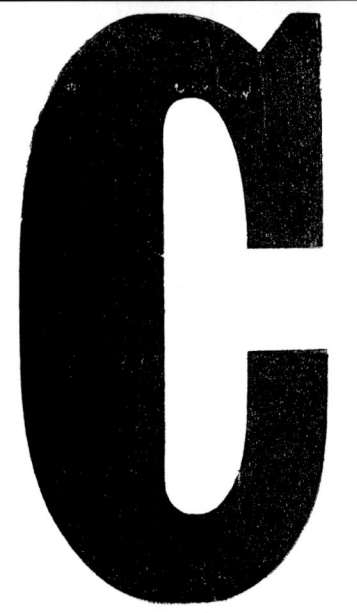

Polly Staple — Curator

CUBITT Gallery
8 Angel Mews
London N1 9HH

T +44 (0)20 7278 8226
F +44 (0)20 7278 2544
E polly@cubittartists.org.uk
www.cubittartists.org.uk

<u>Design</u>
A2-Graphics/SW/HK

<u>For</u>
Cubitt Gallery_
Art gallery_
London, UK

<u>Info</u>
Relocating to a former print workshop provided the inspiration
for a bold, one-colour identity for this artists' collective. A
different letterpress "C" is used for each new exhibition invitation,
and consequently applied to stationery; the identity is highly
recognizable yet fluid.

**VALUE and
SERVICE**

**20 CHARLES ROWAN HOUSE
MARGERY STREET
LONDON WC1X 0EH**
TEL/FAX: +44 (0)20 7689 4526
WWW.VALUEANDSERVICE.CO.UK
PARTNERS: SEAN MURPHY
AND HAZEL RATTIGAN

**VALUE and
SERVICE**

**20 CHARLES ROWAN HOUSE
MARGERY STREET
LONDON WC1X 0EH**
TEL/FAX: +44 (0)20 7689 4526
WWW.VALUEANDSERVICE.CO.UK
HAZEL RATTIGAN
HAZEL@VALUEANDSERVICE.CO.UK
+44 (0)7966 401 758

**VALUE and
SERVICE**

**20 CHARLES ROWAN HOUSE
MARGERY STREET
LONDON WC1X 0EH**
TEL/FAX: +44 (0)20 7689 4526
WWW.VALUEANDSERVICE.CO.UK
SEAN MURPHY
SEAN@VALUEANDSERVICE.CO.UK
+44 (0)7958 637 033

Design
Value and Service
Sean Murphy_
Hazel Rattigan

For
Value and Service_
Designers_
London, UK

Info
Antiquated card stock and writing paper (ranging from old-
skool luxury to basic and aged) is sourced from stationers,
newsagents and flea markets before being sent to the printers.
Contact details are added via gloss-black foil-blocking;
the contrast is acute.

fanny khoo
ART DIRECTOR_COPYWRITER

....

:: FLINK ::
de burburestraat 20
2000 antwerpen

....

fanny@flink.be
www.flink.be

....

t. 03/227.06.53
f. 03/226.96.92

<u>Design</u>
Flink
 Fanny Khoo_
 Tom Merckx

<u>For</u>
 Flink_
 Designers_
 Antwerp, Belgium

<u>Info</u>
At Flink, a team of "evolving pattern makers" personally
combine a typeface, box shape and background pattern
for their cards, the idea being to differentiate while remaining
part of the whole.

Design
Karen Jane

For
Karen Jane_
Designer_
London, UK

Info
A prolific logo designer, Karen's series of logo sticker-cards allows her to present a constantly updated portfolio. The template stays the same, though, and may also be used to showcase other series.

Design
 Duffy
 Adam Whitaker

For
 English_
 Advertising agency_
 London, UK

Info
 An intricate heraldic logo, printed using gold foil-blocking on
 beer-mat board, hints at less predictable elements of Englishness.

laVista
comunicació visual

Frederic Mompou 6. 9º
08005 Barcelona

Angela Broggi
Patrick Thomas

laVista
comunicació visual

T +34 932 21 26 56
M 607 601 384
M 607 601 385

lavista@lavistadesign.com

www.lavistadesign.com

Frederic Mompou 6. 9º
08005 Barcelona

Angela Broggi

laVista
comunicació visual

T +34 932 21 26 56
M 607 601 384

angela@lavistadesign.com

www.lavistadesign.com

Design
  laVista
   Angela Broggi_
   Patrick Thomas

For
  laVista
   Designers_
   Barcelona, Spain

Info
A white card with red type is overprinted with black; the company name and relevant information for each version being left "white out". The stock is heavy and matt coated so as to withstand the large-scale overprinting. Hailing from Barcelona, the cards are in three languages: English, Spanish and Catalan.

laVista
comunicació visual
comunicación visual

T +34 932 21 26 56

lavista@lavistadesign.com

www.lavistadesign.com

Angela Broggi
Patrick Thomas

laVista
comunicació visual

T +34 932 21 26 56
M 607 601 384
M 607 601 385

lavista@lavistadesign.com

www.lavistadesign.com

Ptge Masoliver 25. 2°

08005 Barcelona

Patrick Thomas

laVista

visual communication

T +34 932 21 26 56

M 607 601 385

patrick@lavistadesign.com
www.lavistadesign.com

tinaborg melbourne

Design
Clear
Matthew McCarthy

For
Tina Borg_
Fashion designer_
Melbourne,
Australia

Info
Renowned for her collections of radical clothes in subtle blacks,
Tina's architectural inspiration generated the overlaid,
bitmapped images. Printed in metallic black and UV varnish
on a plastic stock, textural and tonal variations add to the mix.

<u>Design/photography</u> <u>For</u>
12k   12k_
Taylor Deupree   Designer_
                     New York, USA

<u>Info</u>
Taylor Deupree makes digital music, runs several record labels and designs the accompanying graphics. On this card, as with the wider identity, an understated combination of abstracted photography, meandering line and minimal type mirror the ambience of Taylor's musical output.

www. automatic- design.com

automatic
top floor
100 de beauvoir road
london n1 4en
t 020 7923 4857
f 020 7923 4853
ben@automatic-design.com
www.automatic-design.com
ben tibbs partner

<u>Design</u>
Automatic
Martin Carty_
Ben Tibbs

<u>For</u>
Automatic_
Designers_
London, UK

<u>Info</u>
Thin, lightweight, waterproof and flexible; this collage of photographic and digital imagery is printed on to futuristic plastic paper.

Design
  Schwipe

For
  Schwipe_
  Designers/
  clothing label_
  Melbourne,
  Australia

Info
  Schwipe's anarchic t-shirt graphics often wrap around the body;
  similarly, the acid-coloured, hand-rendered logo runs from front
  to back around this card.

SNEAKER FREAKER MAGAZINE

PO BOX 1571, COLLINGWOOD, 3066, AUSTRALIA

WOODY

PH/FX (613) 9416 9393
MB 0402 352 485

WOODY@SNEAKERFREAKER.COM
WWW.SNEAKERFREAKER.COM

Design
Big Block Creative

For
Sneaker Freaker_
Magazine_
Melbourne,
Australia

Info
An unusually irreverent magazine, dedicated to the obsession
some have with their trainers; it requires an equally loud card.

pmcb

MERIEL SCOTT
PARTNER
PRECIOUS MCBANE   T + 44 (0)20 7729 2213
ART & DESIGN PARTNERSHIP F + 44 (0)20 7729 1292
50 FLORIDA STREET   M 07970 533 007
LONDON E2 6AE   E mail4.preciousmcbane.com

Design
Eyefood

For
Precious McBane_
Furniture/interior
designers_
London, UK

Info
Simple two-colour printing is used to maximum effect,
reproducing the "all-over" pmcb pattern.

50

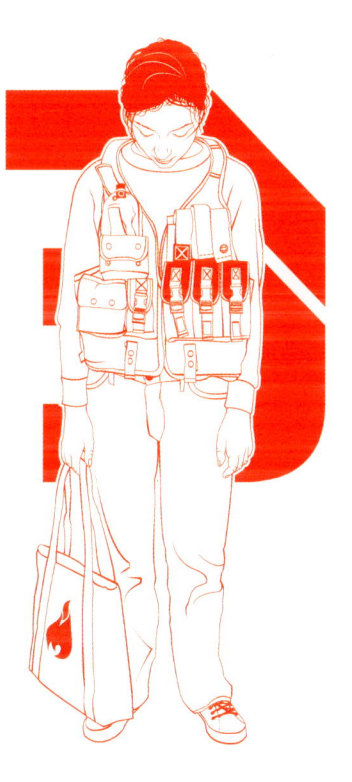

GRAPHIC DESIGN. MULTIMEDIA. ILLUSTRATION.
PRODUCT. CREATIVE THOUGHT.

BURN.   T. 0151 707 6707
254 LIVERPOOL PALACE.   F. 0151 708 5050
9 SLATER STREET, LIVERPOOL.   E. INFO@BURNEVERYTHING.CO.UK
L1 4BW, UNITED KINGDOM.   W. BURNEVERYTHING.CO.UK

Design
 Burn
 David Hand_
 Sam Wiehl

For
 Burn_
 Designers_
 Liverpool, UK

Info
 Combining line illustration with an original symbol and
 logotype, this card showcases a variety of styles to the extent
 that it is referred to as "promotional literature" by the designers.

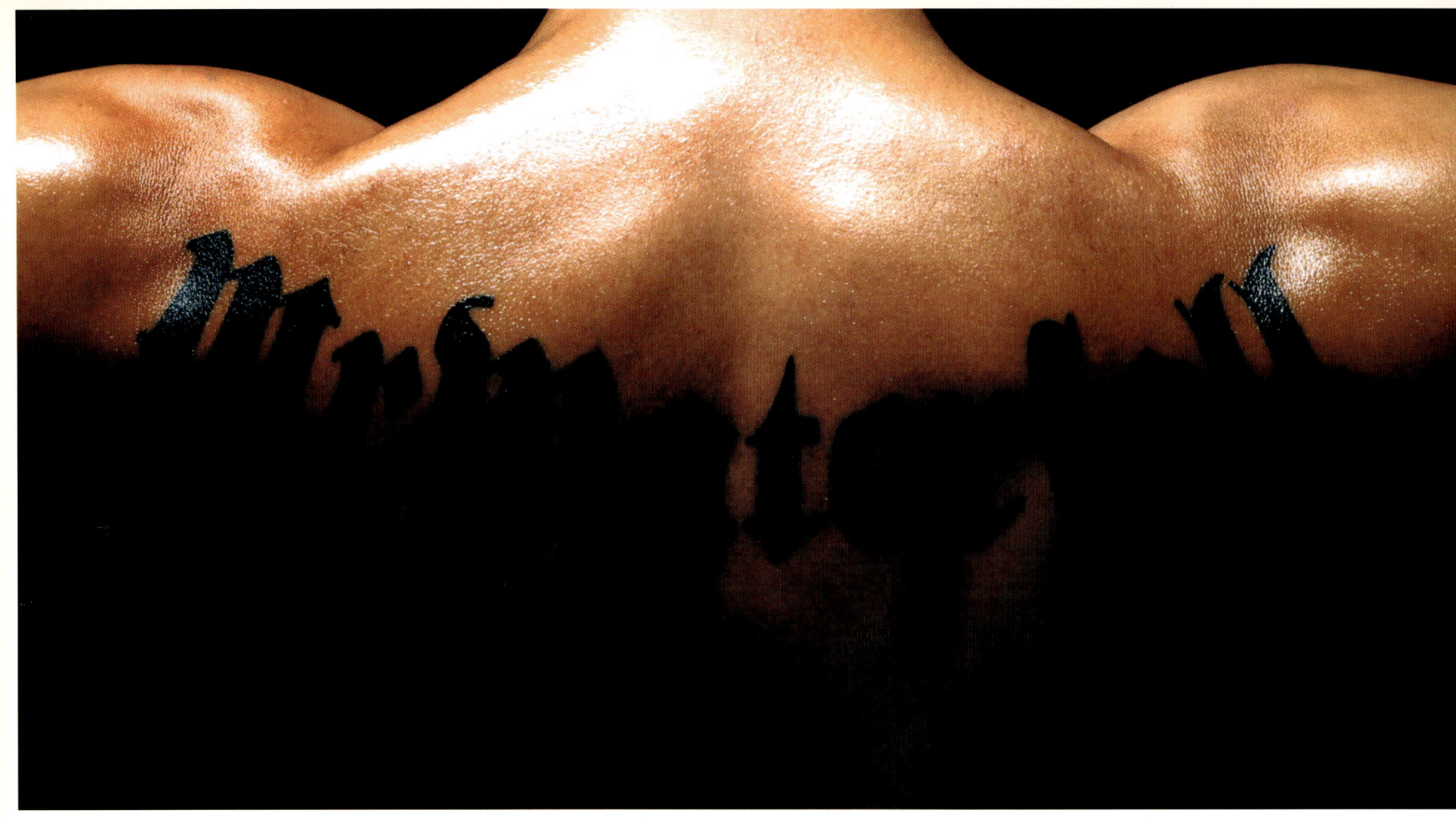

Design
 Simon Waterfall
Photography
 Matt Mitchell
Tattoo
 Alex Binnie

For
 Simon Waterfall_
 Art director_
 London, UK

Info
Known for his bold statements and unshrinking personality,
the choice of type on Simon's enigmatic business card inspired
another personal statement, this time rendered upon his
own skin.

simon@waterfall.co.uk

simon waterfall.   .

GARY BENZEL

809 F STREET
SAN DIEGO, CA 92101
619 234-5855
619 234-5719 FAX
GARY@GREENLADY.COM

GL
GREEN LADY

Design
Green Lady
Gary Benzel_
Todd St John

For
Green Lady_
Designers/
clothing label_
San Diego/
New York, USA

Info
On one side the image is of a distressed card, having been
crumpled up and discarded; on the other it looks as if it has
been found, smoothed out and given a second glance.

FULL SUPER GRAPHIC 100% 100% 100%

BRETT GRAPHIC PLUS

Graphical **engineering** phone:+49(0)431-5.70.37.54

Marc Fiebelkorn

publisher & chief-instructor
redaktion BRETT, jahnstraße 10, 24116 kiel
tel. 0431-5703754 / fax 0431-5703756
email: m.fiebelkorn@brettmag.de
BRETT Graphic Plus, jahnstraße 10, 24116 kiel

Design
 BRETT Graphic Plus
 Marc Fiebelkorn

For
 BRETT Graphic Plus_
 Designer/publisher_
 Kiel, Germany

Info
 BRETT Graphic Plus magazine plays with the language of
 mechanics' manuals, speed-dials and go-faster stripes, offering
 "graphical engineering" on tap.

Design
Heightlab
Chris Hutchinson

For
Heightlab
Designer_
Los Angeles, USA

Info
Onwards and upwards; a fun combination of arrows and tall things (ascenders and giraffes) accentuates this company's name.

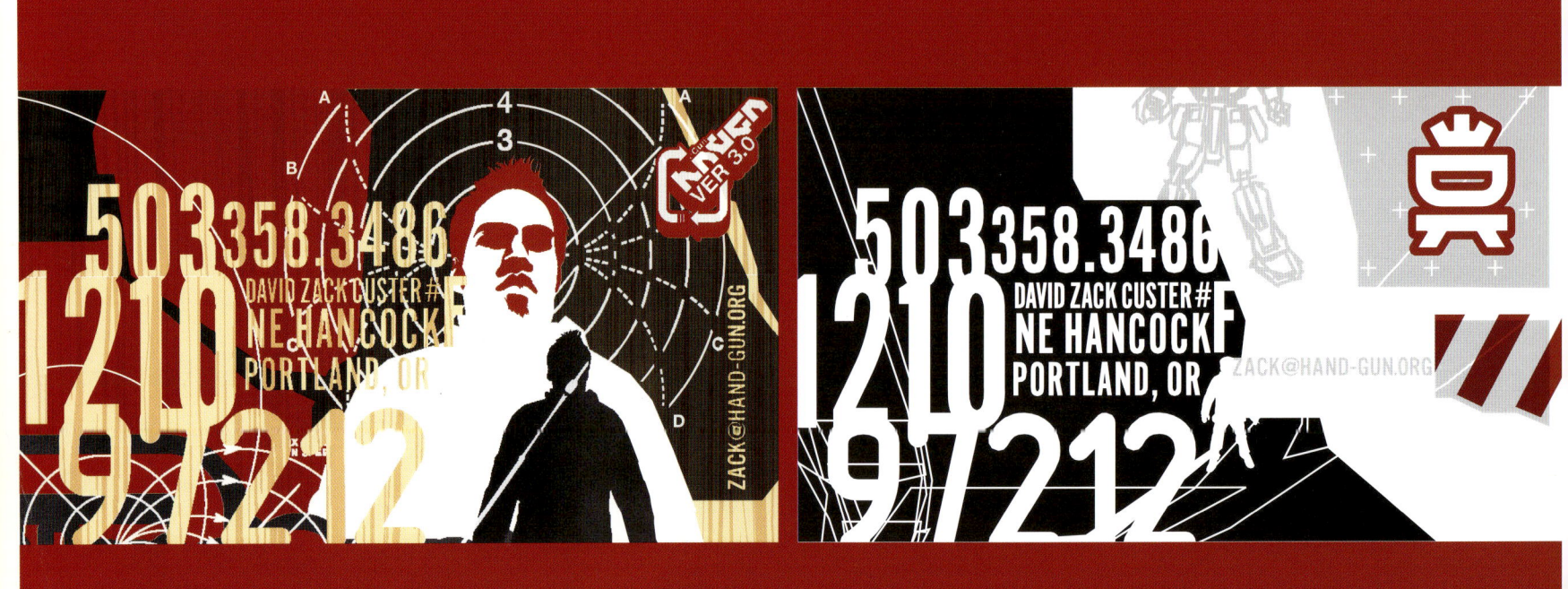

Design
HandGun
David Zack Custer

For
HandGun_
Designer_
Portland, USA

Info
A collage of elements lifted from various graphic languages,
shown business-card size, presents a boiled-down world view.

Design
  David Carson

For
  David Carson_
  Designer_
  Los Angeles/
  New York/
  Charleston, USA

Info
  Although it is printed in classic black on white, design maverick
  David Carson pushes the boundaries of legibility with this card.
  Chaotic elements, redolent of mangled clip-art and abstract
  mark-making, are isolated and re-mixed alongside relevant
  information to be re-presented in several versions.

ADAM@REGULARPRODUCT.COM

THINK BIG STAY SMALL
(GIMME A CALL)

THINK OF EVERYTHING AT ONCE ALL OF THE TIME

TRUST US. WE LOVE YOU.

Design
 Regular Product

For
 Regular Product _
 Designer_
 Sydney, Australia

Info
 Adam of Regular Product views his cards as "left-over public
 service announcements".

NF
NOFUTURE

WWW.NFCOMMUNITY.COM

 ON NOW ❤️ K.

X-DREEM ®
xdreem@prodigy.net

NF ®
O
WWW.NFCOMMUNITY.COM

the x-dreem corporation.
16 Manhattan avenue #1F.
Brooklyn, NEW YORK 11206 USA.
phone #1-718-218-9399
facks #1-718-218-6611
xdreem@prodigy.net
dave denis; main—
man—

dave denis
main man + stuff maker
16 manhattan avenue #1F.
BROOKLYN, NY 11206 USA
phone #1-718-218-9399 • facks #718-218-6611

Design
Dave Denis

For
Dave Denis_
Designer_
New York, USA

Info
Artist, illustrator, fashion designer and entrepreneur, Dave's
individuality is emphasized via his unique handwriting,
which is printed in raised thermographic ink.

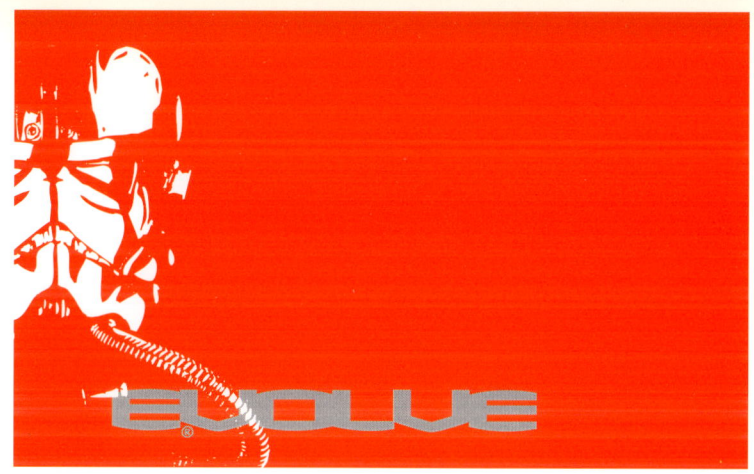

Design
 Josh Van Lammeren_
 Scott Holding

For
 Evolve
 Skate shop_
 Melbourne,
 Australia

Info
An obsession with sci-fi provides rich source material
for this series of slick cards.

Design
Josh Van Lammeren

For
Evolve
Skate shop_
Melbourne,
Australia

Info
The illustration on this store-card, depicting how skateboard design has evolved and streamlined, implies that this shop's been around since the early days.

www.evolve214.com

EVOLVE 214 Chapel St. Prahran Melbourne, Australia 3181

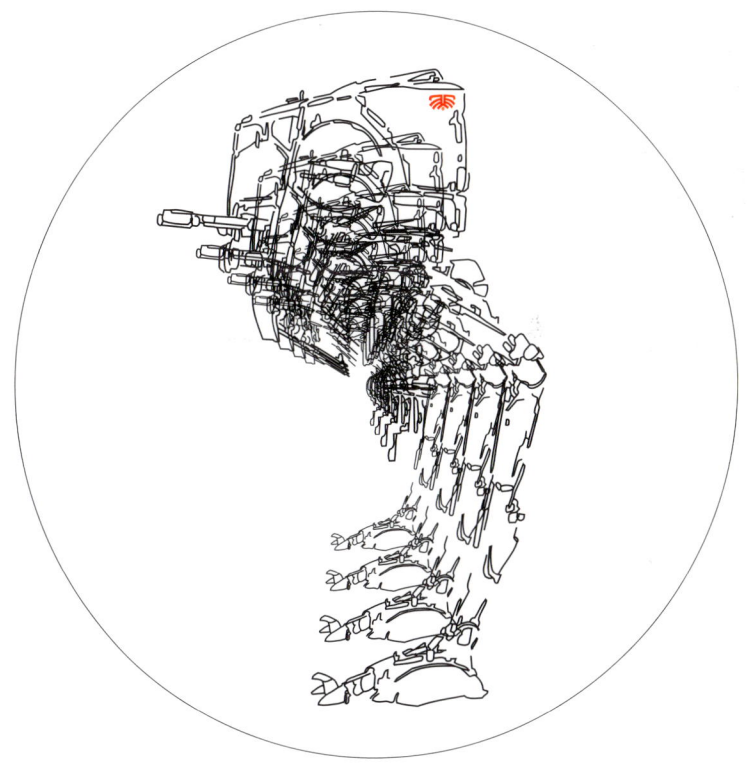

Design
  Josh Van Lammeren_
  Scott Holding
Illustration
  David Nissani

For
  Evolve
  Skate shop_
  Melbourne,
  Australia

Info
This attention-grabbing, die-cut card was inspired by "Star Wars" aesthetics, and hints at the personal obsessions of the Evolve team.

Design/illustration
StolenSpace
Richard Hennings

For
StolenSpace_
Designer/illustrator_
London, UK

Info
Based on the iconic "hello my name is" badge, the two versions of this sticker-card may be personalized by adding tags or doodles. Peel off and stick around town to spread the word.

Unit 4, N° 11 St Philips Road, Surbiton, Surrey. KT6 4DU
T: 020 8390 6468 E: info@stolenspace.com

Unit 4, N° 11 St Philips Road, Surbiton, Surrey. KT6 4DU
T: 020 8390 6468 E: info@stolenspace.com

Design/illustration
Jon Burgerman

For
Jon Burgerman_
Illustrator_
Nottingham, UK

Info
Mounted on corrugated cardboard, Jon's cards are also stickers,
each sporting a distinctly cheeky character.

Design
Josh Welsher

For
To Die For_
Clothing label_
Los Angeles, USA

Info
To Die For create t-shirts, accessories and graphics using a mix of graffiti techniques and hot-rod styling. This glossy black card is totally rock'n'roll.

Design
Toko Chan

For
Japanize_
Magazine_
Norwich, UK

Info
With cards printed on a bright, uncoated stock similar to that used for the cover of her zine, Toko, a Japanese illustrator living in England, depicts herself and her world as cute, crazy and a touch surreal.

Miles Murray Sorrell FUEL®

33 Fournier Street
Spitalfields
London E1 6QE
Telephone **020 7377 2697**   Fax   **020 7247 4697**

fuel@fuel-design.com

Design
 Miles Murray Sorrell
 FUEL
Painting
 Gordon Murray

For
 Miles Murray Sorrell
 FUEL_
 Designers_
 London, UK

Info
 The latest in Fuel's line of portraiture cards, this group image,
 posed in their studio, was painted by the father of one of the team.

TWResearch

5 Cowcross Street
London EC1M 6DW

T. 020 7324 9999
F. 020 7324 9980
terry@twresearch.com
www.twresearch.com

TWResearch

5 Cowcross Street
London EC1M 6DW

T. 020 7324 9999
F. 020 7324 9980
terry@twresearch.com
www.twresearch.com

TWResearch

5 Cowcross Street
London EC1M 6DW

T. 020 7324 9999
F. 020 7324 9980
terry@twresearch.com
www.twresearch.com

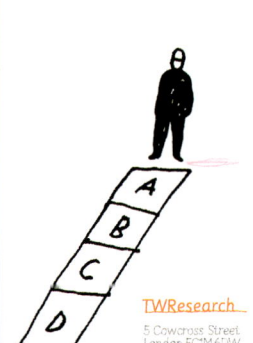

TWResearch

5 Cowcross Street
London EC1M 6DW

T. 020 7324 9999
F. 020 7324 9980
terry@twresearch.com
www.twresearch.com

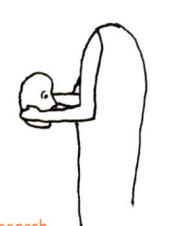

TWResearch

5 Cowcross Street
London EC1M 6DW

T. 020 7324 9999
F. 020 7324 9980
terry@twresearch.com
www.twresearch.com

Terry
Watkins

Managing Director

Terry Watkins

Managing Director

Design
 Kerr Noble
Illustration
 Paul Davis

For
 TWResearch_
 Market research
 agency_
 London, UK

Info
Working with idiosyncratic illustrator Paul Davis, Kerr Noble
created a cast of twelve characters to inhabit their client's
"world", a place where media meets culture. Each staffer gets
all twelve cards, and as an ice-breaker they are a great
success, with clients begging for complete sets.

dakota brown

www.3st.com
2043 w. wabansia av
chicago.il.60647

ph: 773.384.8888
fx: " " .8855
dakota@3st2.com

professional
designer

THIRST

THIRST
DESIGN
MEAT
MARKET

3ST.COM

EWA SARNACKA
INSPEKTOR No 420

2043 WABANSIA
CHICAGO IL 60647
T: 773.384.8888
F: 773.384.8855
E: EWA@3ST2.COM

RICH
RICH@3ST2.COM

THIRST
2043 w. wabansia
CHICAGO IL
773-384-8888
773-384-8855
WWW.3ST.COM

Barbara Valicenti
Thirst
132 W. Station Street
Barrington, IL 60010

T> 847·842·0222
F> 847·842·0220
E> barb@3st2.com
www.3st.com

"Keeping business in the black"

>Rob Wittig
>thirst
>rob@3st2.com
>2043 W. Wabansia Ave
>Chicago, IL 60647
>vox 773.384.8888
>fax 773.384.8855
>www.3st.com

rick V.ALICENTI
THIRST

rick@3st2.com
www.3st.com $
1.847.842.0222

CHICAGO + BARRINGTON

Design
  Thirst
  Dakota Brown_
  Rich Hanson_
  Ewa Sarnacka_
  Barbara Valicenti_
  Rick Valicenti_
  Rob Wittig

For
  Thirst_
  Designers_
  Chicago, USA

Info
Each member of this creative studio makes their own mark;
within the boundaries of a small "black and white" card they
create aesthetically diverse worlds.

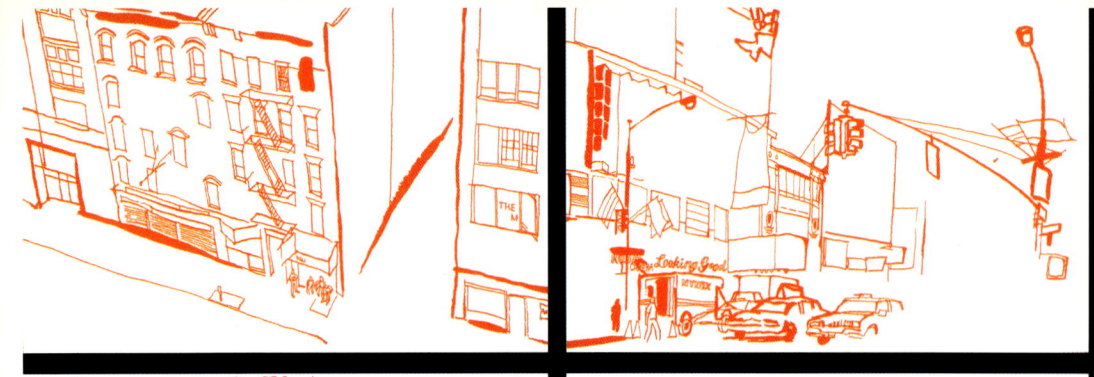

Lucinda Rogers

75 Columbia Road, London E2 7RG
Telephone/Fax +44 (0)20 7729 9517
e.mail lucindadot@hotmail.com

Design
 Julian Morey
Illustration
 Lucinda Rogers

For
 Lucinda Rogers_
 Illustrator_
 London, UK

Info
 An acclaimed illustrator specializing in urban landscapes,
 Lucinda features New York, one of her favourite cities, on
 her set of cards. Rendered in vibrant orange, on stock which
 approximates water-colour paper, it's as if she has put her
 brush down and cut off a corner, just for you.

space3eindhoven
Grafische & Illustratieve Ontwerpen

Joost van der Heijden

Kerkstraat 24
5611 GJ Eindhoven

Postbus 8007
5601 KA Eindhoven

T. +31 (0)40 213 53 82
F. +31 (0)40 213 53 75
E. joost@space3.nl

Design
Space3

For
Space3_
Designers_
Eindhoven,
The Netherlands

Info
Mark-making by hand and computer, layers of information and some overt branding (the appropriation of the "Brownie" salute for instance), add up to an exuberant card for these street-inspired designers and illustrators.

Design
Burn
David Hand_
Sam Wiehl

For_
Burn_
Designers_
Liverpool, UK

Design
Burn
David Hand_
Sam Wiehl

For
Burn_
Designers_
Liverpool, UK

Info
Large square formats are used for both of these cards which
showcase the wide range of Burn's image-making techniques.

I'd look good
on you.

quickhoney.com

QuickHoney

"We spent the rest of the day together and ended up doing it all over again on the beach, but this time it was a silent fuck. We exchanged phone numbers at his insistence, saying he was in love with me (what a geek). He gave me his number and I was going to give him mine but I changed my mind at the last minute and made up a phoney number. He was good, but there's always better."

718.222.0127

Tell me...how is your
girlfriend doing?

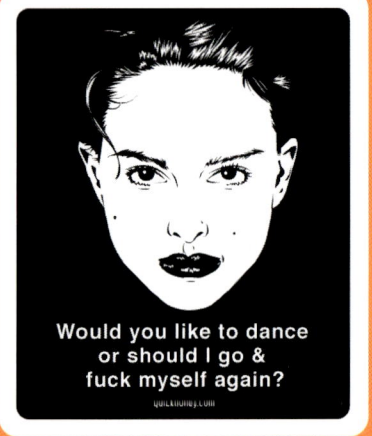

Would you like to dance
or should I go &
fuck myself again?

QUICKHONEY.COM

Design
   QuickHoney

For
   QuickHoney_
   Designers_
   New York, USA

Info
Rendering pin-up celebrities and girls about town in their
signature graphic style, QuickHoney's cards are instantly
attractive. Collect the set. The over-blown, pixellated burger
on the reverse makes you think of that other great pleasure.

Smile if you want to sleep with me.

quickhoney.com

You're ugly, but you interest me.

quickhoney.com

Your place or mine?

quickhoney.com

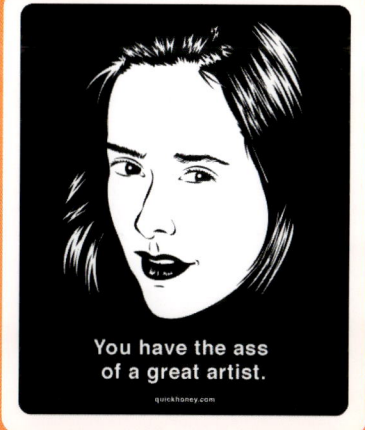

You have the ass of a great artist.

quickhoney.com

ra@ala.ch

www.ala.ch

ala webstatt & chmork.net
Alexandra Ramildi
Rotbuchstrasse 22, 8037 Zurich/CH
T+41 1 364 2750, F+41 1 364 2751

rek@ala.ch

www.ala.ch

ala webstatt & chmork.net
René Etienne Keller
Rotbuchstrasse 22, 8037 Zurich/CH
T+41 1 364 2757, F+41 1 364 2751

Design
 Ala Webstatt &
 Chmork.net
 René Etienne Keller_
 Alexandra Ramildi

For
 Ala Webstatt &
 Chmork.net_
 Designers_
 Zurich, Switzerland

Info
 Staffers at this computer-friendly image-making studio
 are depicted on their cards as cute c-g-icons.

Marcus Charalambos
Producer - XY Music
Tel 020 7204 1931

marcus@xynetwork.com

Cheryl Davies
Researcher
Tel 020 7204 1965

cheryl.davies@xynetwork.com

Lynne Pritchard
Webmistress
Tel 020 7204 1952

lynne.pritchard@xynetwork.com

Paul Bennun
Director
Tel 020 7204 1921
Mob 0771 414 5830

paul.bennun@xynetwork.com

Ben Cave
Assistant Producer - XY Music
Tel 020 7204 1948
Mob 07967 003168

ben.cave@xynetwork.com

Claire Neal
Researcher / Broadcast assistant
Tel 020 7204 1967
Mob 07944 533 942

claire.neal@xynetwork.com

Jez Nelson
Director
Tel 020 7204 1920

jez@xynetwork.com

Steve Ackerman
Outputmeister
Tel 020 7204 1939

steve.ackerman@xynetwork.com

Christine de Leon
Project Manager
Tel 020 7204 1961

christine@xynetwork.com

XY⁴ NETWORK

Units 1-4
1a Old Nichol Street
London
E2 7HR

Fax 020 7739 9799
Tel 020 7613 3211
www.xynetwork.com

Design
Airside

For
XY Network_
Radio production
company_
London, UK

Info
Each member of XY Network chose an icon from the Airside-
designed website to be printed in their favourite colour, in a
square "pixel" format.

Frédérique Daubal
haarlemmerdijk 31 1floor
1013 ka amsterdam the netherlands
tel: +31 (0)20 427 4907
mobile: +31 (0)6 18 05 02 53
www.daubal.com
frederique@daubal.com

<u>Design</u>
Frédérique Daubal
Mario Guay

<u>For</u>
Frédérique Daubal_
Designer_
Amsterdam,
The Netherlands

<u>Info</u>
Mixing pattern, colour and form, Frédérique's card hints at
her creative cross-over between graphic and fashion design.

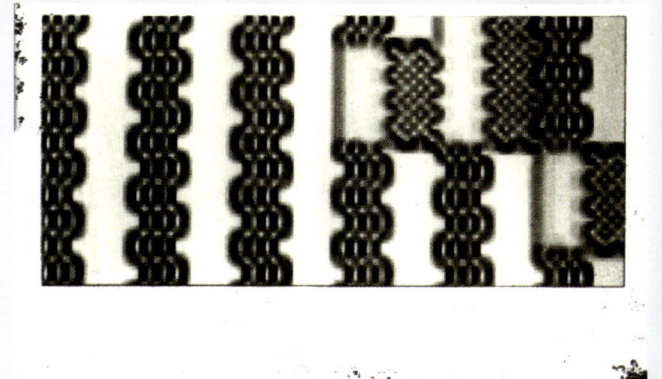

markus reichenbach.moiré

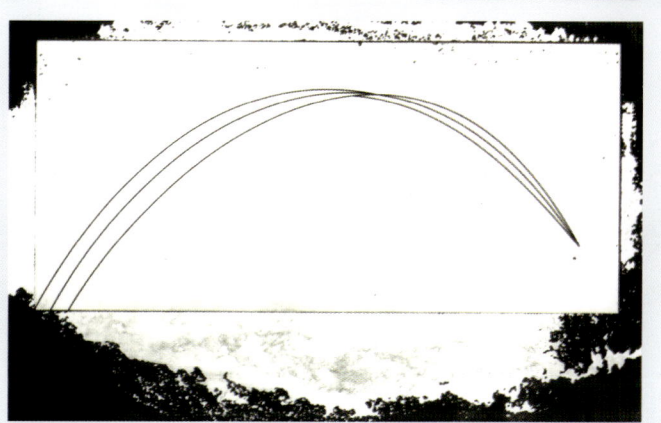

marc kappeler
hardturmstr. 102
CH-8005 zürich
079 247 36 60
mkappeler@access.ch

Design
Moiré
Bianca Brunner_
Marc Kappeler_
Markus Reichenbach

For
Moiré_
Designers_
Zurich, Switzerland

Info
Collaging fragments of computer-generated pattern from early software programs next to childlike handwriting, this card is both enigmatic and expressive.

Sarah Gaventa

Scarlet Projects
49-51 Central Street
London EC1V 8AB
T: 0207 490 3453
F: 0207 336 6861
M: 07968 184469
sarah@scarletprojects.com

Claire Catterall

Scarlet Projects
49-51 Central Street
London EC1V 8AB
T: 0207 490 3431
F: 0207 336 6861
claire@scarletprojects.com

Sarah Gaventa

Scarlet Projects
49-51 Central Street
London EC1V 8AB
T: 0207 490 3453
F: 0207 336 6861
M: 07968 184469
sarah@scarletprojects.com

Claire Catterall

Scarlet Projects
49-51 Central Street
London EC1V 8AB
T: 0207 490 3431
F: 0207 336 6861
claire@scarletprojects.com

Sarah Gaventa

Scarlet Projects
49-51 Central Street
London EC1V 8AB
T: 0207 490 3453
F: 0207 336 6861
M: 07968 184469
sarah@scarletprojects.com

Claire Catterall

Scarlet Projects
49-51 Central Street
London EC1V 8AB
T: 0207 490 3431
F: 0207 336 6861
claire@scarletprojects.com

Sarah Gaventa

Scarlet Projects
49-51 Central Street
London EC1V 8AB
T: 0207 490 3453
F: 0207 336 6861
M: 07968 184469
sarah@scarletprojects.com

Claire and Sarah

Scarlet Projects
49-51 Central Street
London EC1V 8AB
T: 0207 490 3430
F: 0207 336 6861
mail@scarletprojects.com

<u>Design</u>
åbäke

<u>For</u>
Scarlet Projects_
Creative
consultants_
London, UK

<u>Info</u>
For these wordsmiths and image gurus, åbäke created nine designs based on the interior patterns of envelopes (which are intended to obscure content); printed them in blue (red was too obvious for a company named Scarlet); and created matt and glossy versions. Patterns ranging from "masculine to feminine" may be selected, appropriate to any occasion.

Patrick Monnier
Graphic designer
Happypets Products

Av. du Tribunal-fédéral 3, 1005 Lausanne
Tél. 021 323 41 30 Nat. 079 362 37 28
Email. happypetsproducts@hotmail.com
Web. www.happypetsproducts.ch

Violène Pont
Graphic designer
Happypets Products

Av. du Tribunal-fédéral 3, 1005 Lausanne
Tel. 021 323 41 30 Nat. 078 744 88 85
Email. happypetsproducts@hotmail.com
Web. www.happypetsproducts.ch

Design
   Happypets
   Products

For
   Happypets
   Products_
   Designers_
   Lausanne,
   Switzerland

Info
As part of an ever-evolving visual identity generated by
studying the relationship between humans and animals,
Happypets' cards relate to colour codes used in the fabrication
of sanitary bags distributed to Swiss dog owners, the aim being
cleaner streets. However "solid" the research, the resultant cards
are enigmatically abstract.

Cédric Henny
Graphic designer
Happypets Products

Av. du Tribunal-fédéral 3, 1005 Lausanne
Tél. 021 323 41 30
Email. happypetsproducts@hotmail.com
Web. www.happypetsproducts.ch

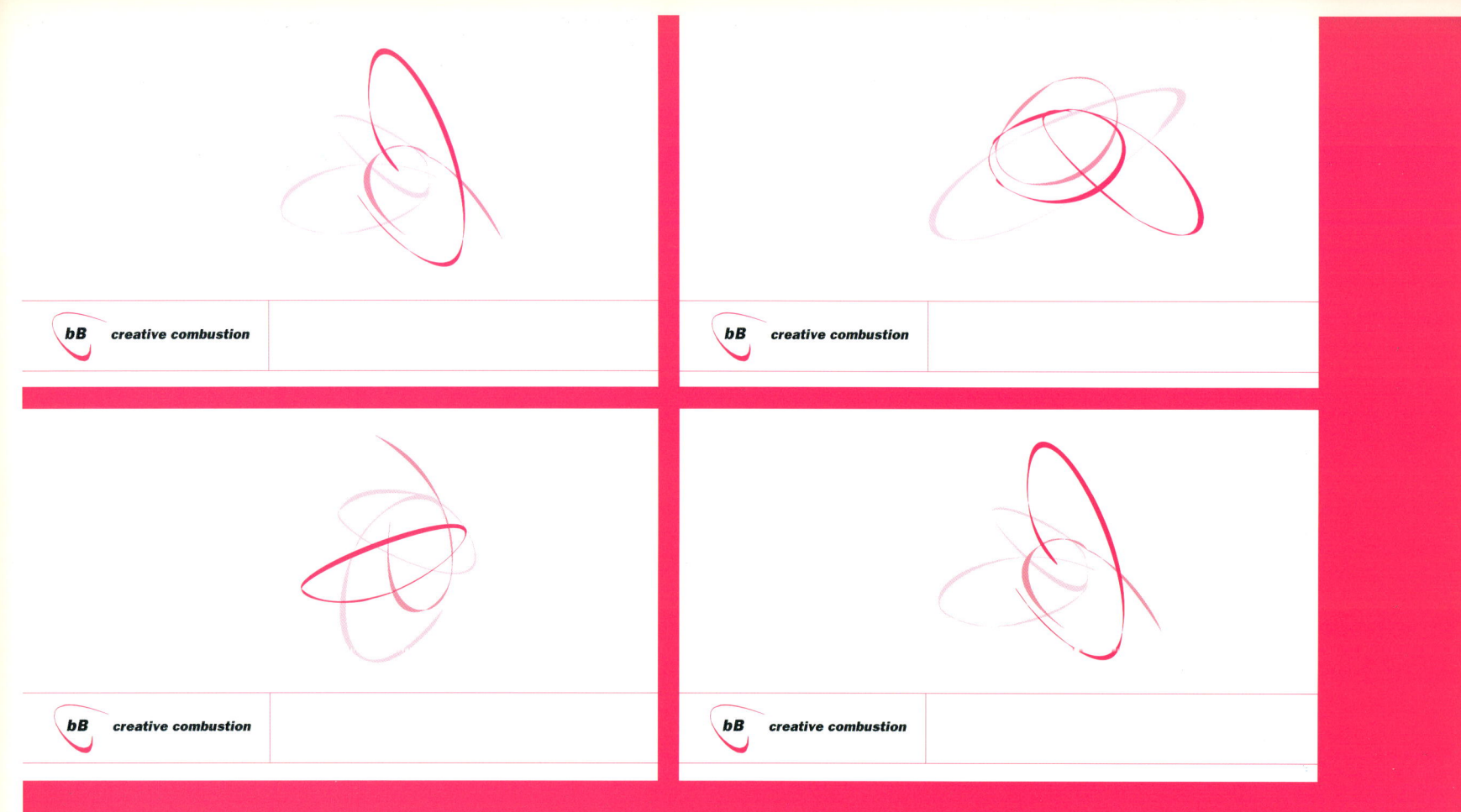

Design
  Move Design

For
  boomBang_
  Design & engineering
  collective_
  San Francisco, USA

Info
  Each independent member of this design and engineering
  collective has their own "schism" mark, denoting "creative
  combustion and constant change"; appropriate enough as
  their business is materials research and product innovation.

PATRICK SUNDQVIST
Senior Designer

T +44 (0)20 7737 7579
F +44 (0)20 7737 7971
M +44 (0)793 266 8451
E patrick@head−newmedia.com

Head New Media   The Bon Marché Building
241-251 Ferndale Road   London SW9 8BJ
www.head-newmedia.com

Design
Head
Jason Holland_
Patrick Sundqvist_
Steve Liddell

For
Head_
New media
designers_
London, UK

Info
Super-subtle variations in tone and form create an evocative
collective identity. Painterly images use the simplest of means –
line, pixel, circle – to produce depth and contrast, while the
brackets of the logo are echoed in die-cut nicks and keylines
on the card's reverse.

Printed in England by
Gavin Martin
Associates Limited

Gary Bird Managing Director

T +44 [0]20 8761 3077
F +44 [0]20 8761 6219
Mobile 07831 861464
E gary@gavinmartin.co.uk

KGM House 26-34 Rothschild Street
West Norwood London SE27 0HQ

<u>Design</u>
NB:Studio

<u>For</u>
Gavin Martin_
Printers_
London, UK

<u>Info</u>
This super-fine image of curved, intersecting lines and the
resultant moirés was designed to show off the card-holder's
technical skills.

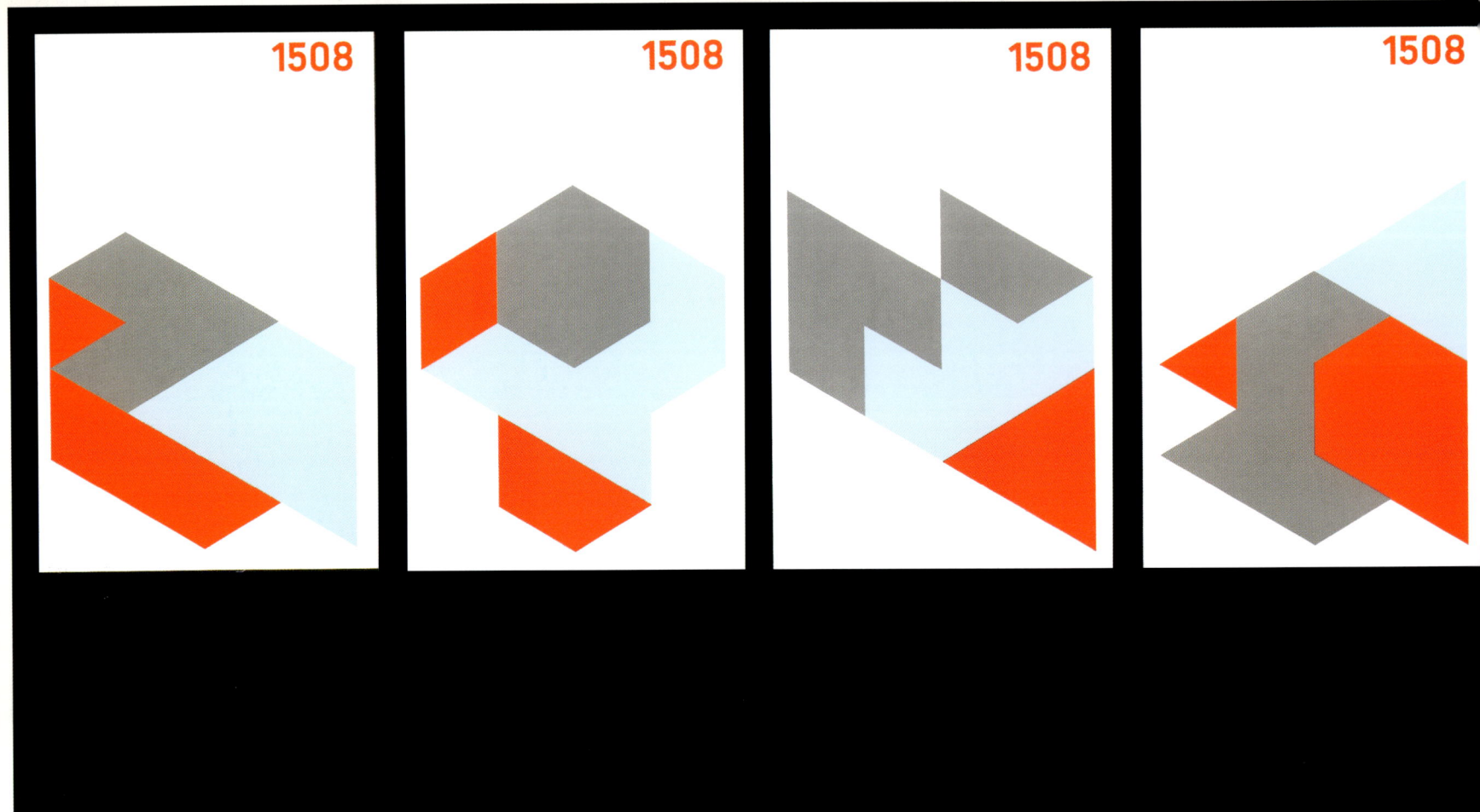

Design
A2-Graphics/SW/HK

For
1508_
Communications
consultants_
Copenhagen,
Denmark

Info
Inspired by Buckminster Fuller's 2-D map of the earth, a new
representation of the five continents was drawn using shapes
that rearrange, connect and unite in new ways; the aim being
to signify this communication company's global reach via their
expertise with new technology.

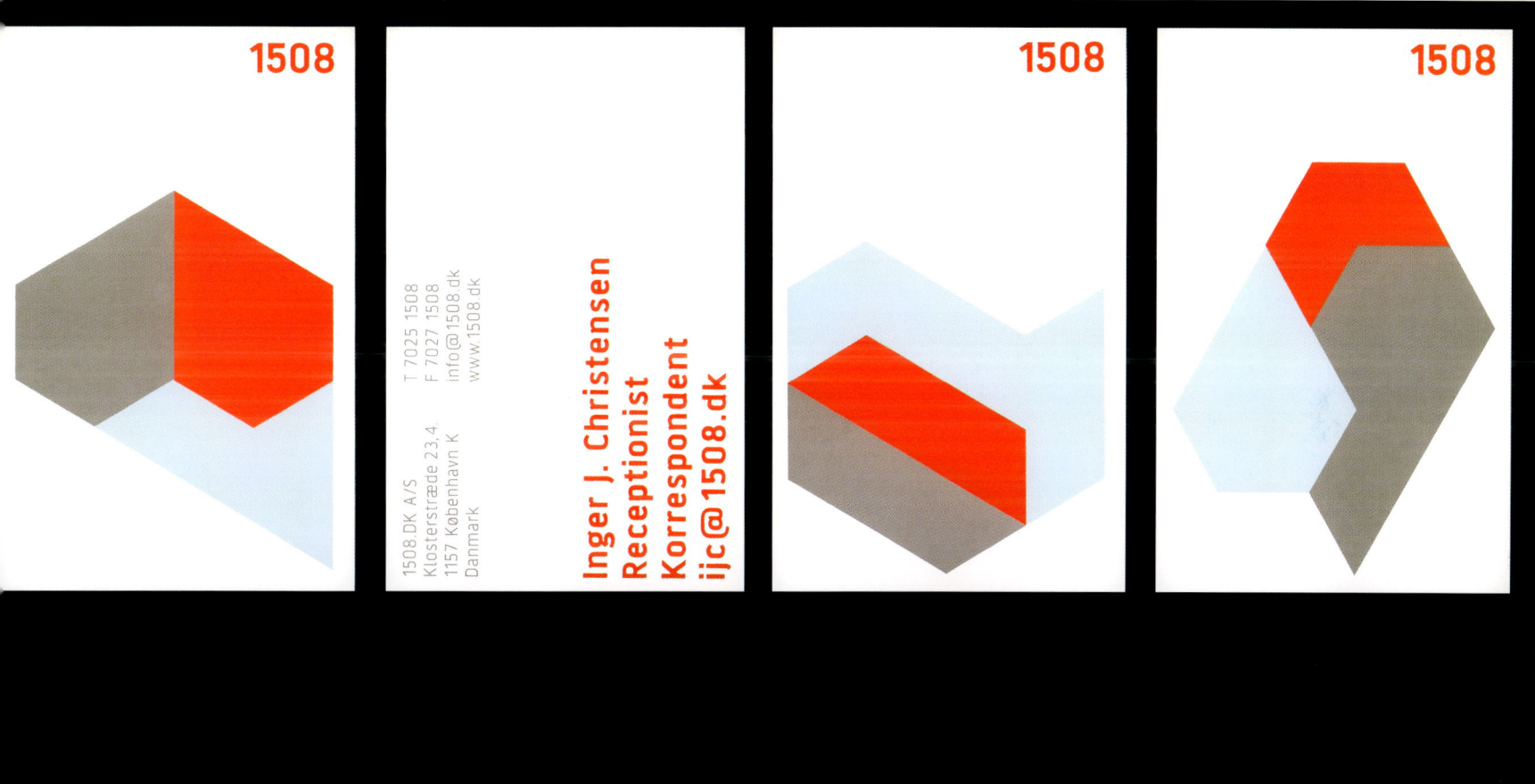

1508

1508 DK A/S
Klosterstræde 23, 4.
1157 København K
Danmark

T 7025 1508
F 7027 1508
info@1508.dk
www.1508.dk

Inger J. Christensen
Receptionist
Korrespondent
ijc@1508.dk

1508

1508

ANDERS W. HANSEN
PROJECT MANAGER

WETWARE

WETWARE A/S
WILDERSGADE 50, 1
1408 COPENHAGEN K
DENMARK

PHONE (+45) 32 54 08 22
WETWARE@WETWARE.DK
WWW.WETWARE.DK

MATHIAS CLAUSEN
ART DIRECTOR

WETWARE

WETWARE A/S
WILDERSGADE 50, 1
1408 COPENHAGEN K
DENMARK

PHONE (+45) 32 54 08 22
WETWARE@WETWARE.DK
WWW.WETWARE.DK

TORBEN JESPERSEN
PARTNER

WETWARE

WETWARE A/S
WILDERSGADE 50, 1
1408 COPENHAGEN K
DENMARK

PHONE (+45) 32 54 08 22
WETWARE@WETWARE.DK
WWW.WETWARE.DK

MICHAEL OVERGAARD
CHIEF EXECUTIVE OFFICER

WETWARE

WETWARE A/S
WILDERSGADE 50, 1
1408 COPENHAGEN K
DENMARK

PHONE (+45) 32 54 08 22
WETWARE@WETWARE.DK
WWW.WETWARE.DK

Design
E-Types

For
Wetware_
Brand consultants_
Copenhagen,
Denmark

Info
If computers have hard- and software, then humans have
"wetware": the brain. This dot.com consultancy was less
techno-obsessed than most, hence the idea to show abstraction,
connection, levels of thought and layers of inspiration, by
means of colour and pattern; all of which is individualized for
each staffer.

Design
Draught Associates
Dave Gibson_
Michael Lenz

For
CC-Lab Limited_
Production
company_
London, UK

Info
For a music production company with many divisions, the idea
was to create a simple visual language for a large family;
staffers are involved in "composing" their image, while the
colours relate them to various specialisms.

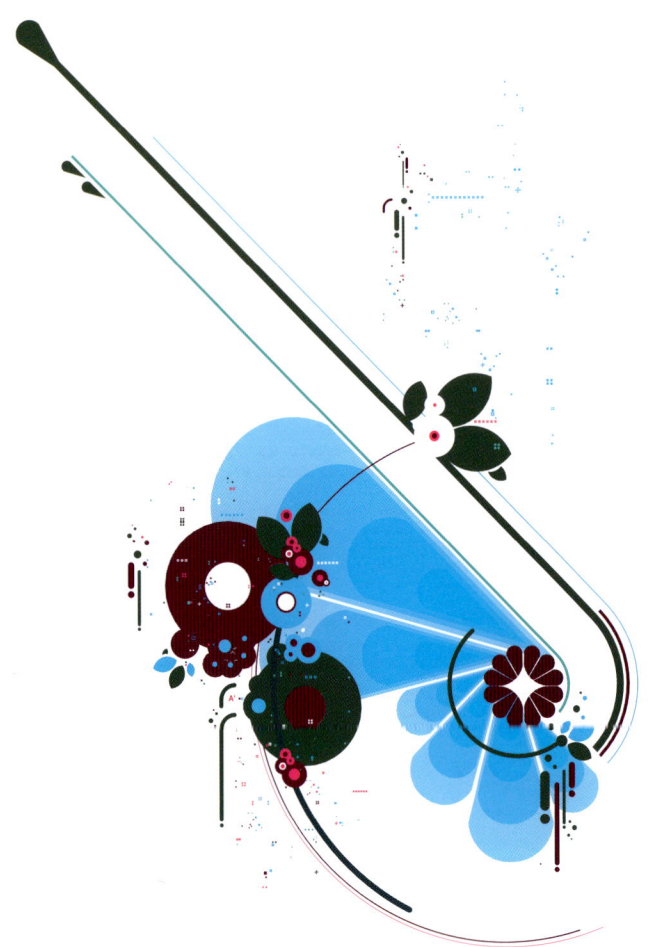

APARTEMENTO 74
Rua Imaculada Conceição, 81
Santa Cecília. 01226-020
São Paulo. Brasil

++ 55.11.3663.1591

www.a-linha.org
clarissa@a-linha.org

Design
A'
Clarissa Tossin

For
A'_
Designer_
São Paulo, Brazil

Info
Designer and illustrator Clarissa Tossin uses her stack of large-format business cards as a mini portfolio; each card features details from a project. At a presentation they act as visual prompts; then you may pick a card.

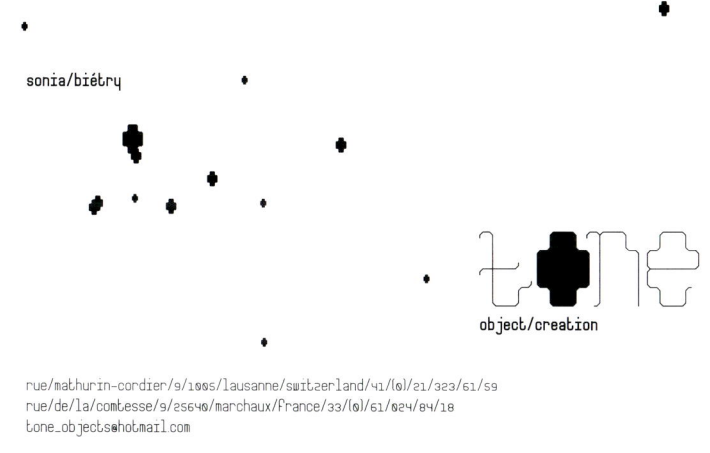

sonia/biétry

tone
object/creation

rue/mathurin-cordier/9/1005/lausanne/switzerland/41/(0)/21/323/61/59
rue/de/la/comtesse/9/25640/marchaux/france/33/(0)/61/024/84/18
tone_objects@hotmail.com

<u>Design</u>
 Happypets
 Products

<u>For</u>
 Tone_
 Industrial designers_
 Lausanne,
 Switzerland/
 Marchaux, France

<u>Info</u>
Combining familiar bitmapped icons with fluid, machine-made
curves and flourishes, Happypets explore the language of
computer-generated design for a partnership of industrial
designers. Differing versions of the image-mix represent each
partner.

Design
 Gasket
 Mike Christoffel_
 Todd Hansson

For
 Gasket_
 Designers_
 Brisbane, Australia

Info
 A set of bold cards in evolving colourways.

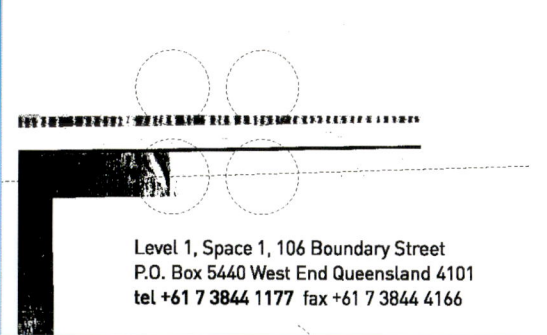

GASKET™

Level 1, Space 1, 106 Boundary Street
P.O. Box 5440 West End Queensland 4101
tel **+61 7 3844 1177** fax **+61 7 3844 4166**

Todd Hansson {0401 134 626}

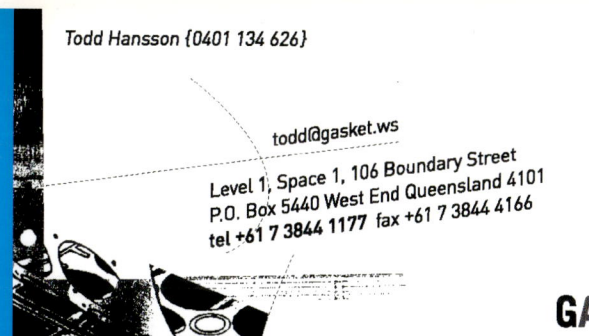

todd@gasket.ws

Level 1, Space 1, 106 Boundary Street
P.O. Box 5440 West End Queensland 4101
tel **+61 7 3844 1177** fax **+61 7 3844 4166**

GASKET™

Michael Christøffel {04 022 38 033}

mike@gasket.ws

Level 1, Space 1, 106 Boundary Street
P.O. Box 5440 West End Queensland 4101
tel **+61 7 3844 1177** fax **+61 7 3844 4166**

GASKET™

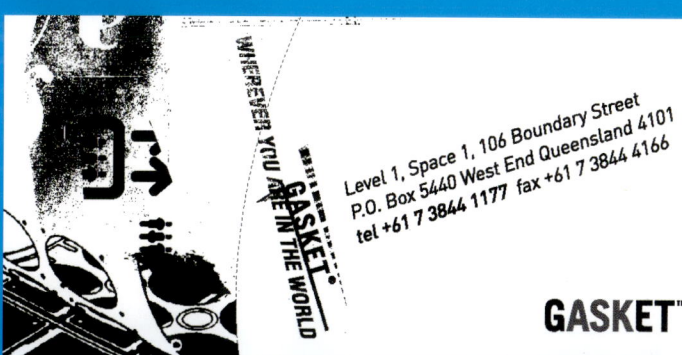

WHEREVER YOU ARE IN THE WORLD

Level 1, Space 1, 106 Boundary Street
P.O. Box 5440 West End Queensland 4101
tel **+61 7 3844 1177** fax **+61 7 3844 4166**

GASKET™

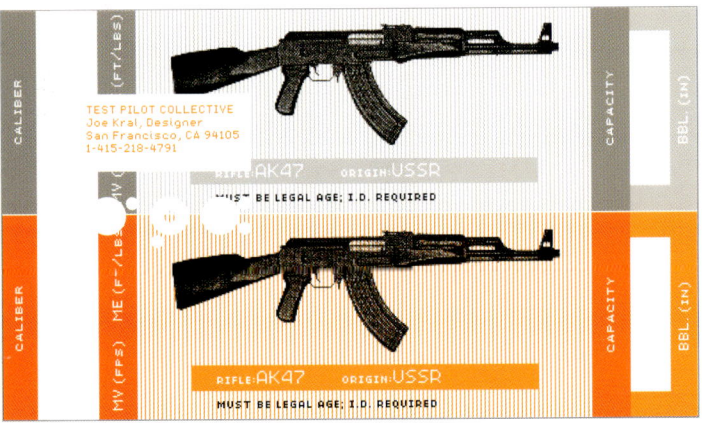

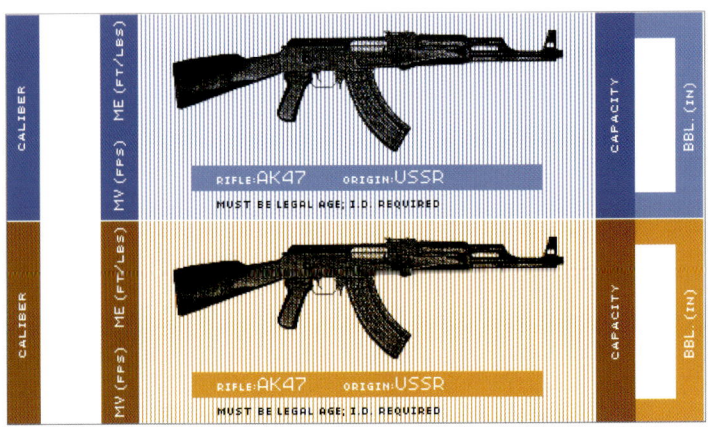

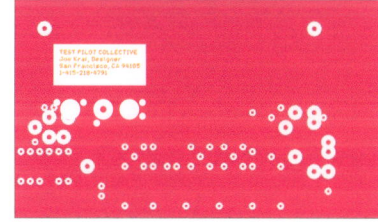
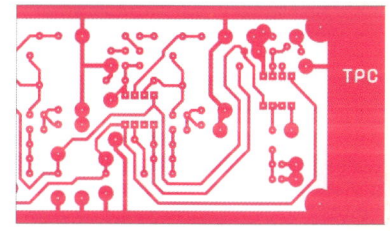
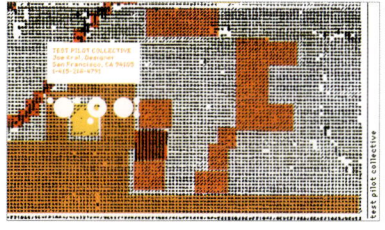
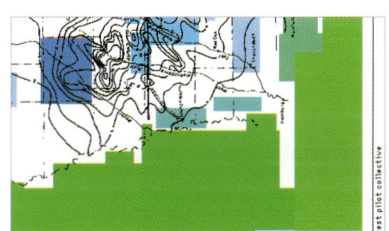

Design/photography
Test Pilot Collective
Joe Kral

For
Test Pilot Collective_
Designers_
San Francisco, USA

Info
Unable to choose a final design for the business card, TPC
decided to unfix the rules. Using desktop technology, a constant
stream of cards, inspired by everyday life – music, people,
places, colours and objects – is produced, the aim being
"to make something that someone will want to keep".

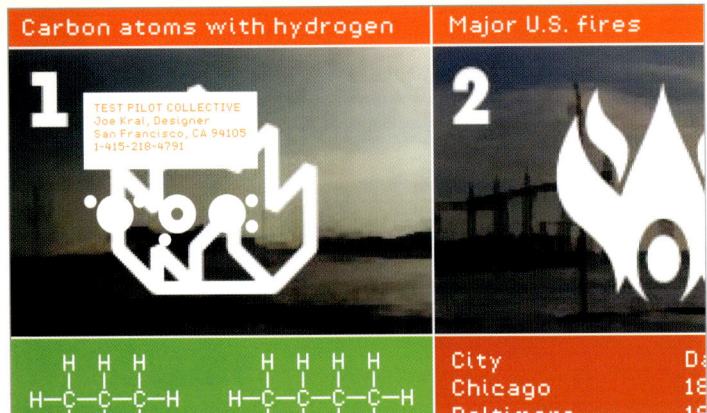

Carbon atoms with hydrogen

1

TEST PILOT COLLECTIVE
Joe Kral, Designer
San Francisco, CA 94105
1-415-218-4791

H H H
H—C—C—C—H

H H H H
H—C—C—C—C—H

Major U.S. fires

2

City   Da
Chicago   18
Baltimore   19

e detector

on-chamber smoke
ector employs
ricium 241, a radio

7

Principal fuel molecule:cellulose

C   C
C—O   C—O   O

TEST PILOT COLLECTIVE
Joe Kral, Designer
San Francisco, CA 94105
1-415-218-4791

Test Pilot
Collective

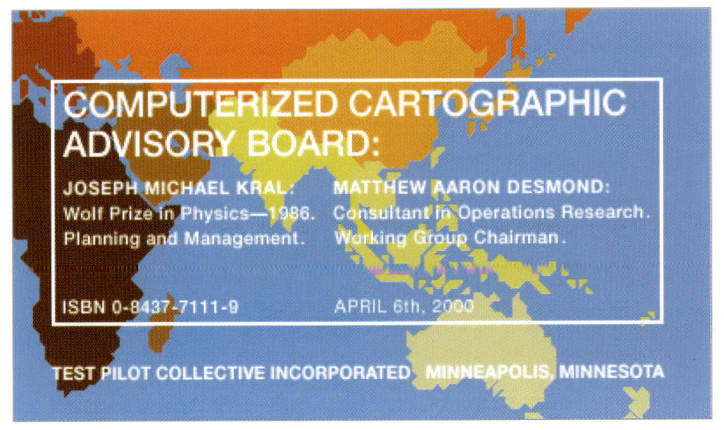

COMPUTERIZED CARTOGRAPHIC ADVISORY BOARD:

JOSEPH MICHAEL KRAL:
Wolf Prize in Physics—1986.
Planning and Management.

MATTHEW AARON DESMOND:
Consultant in Operations Research.
Working Group Chairman.

ISBN 0-8437-7111-9   APRIL 6th, 2000

TEST PILOT COLLECTIVE INCORPORATED   MINNEAPOLIS, MINNESOTA

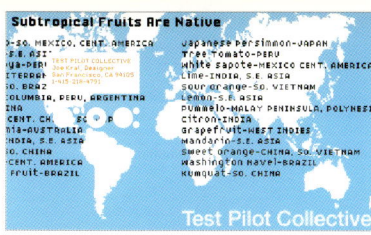

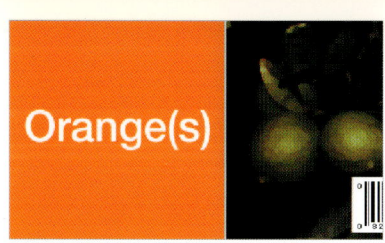

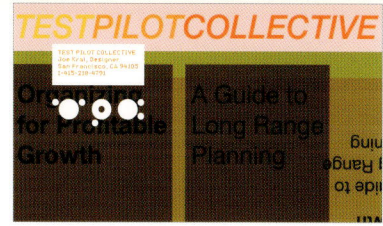

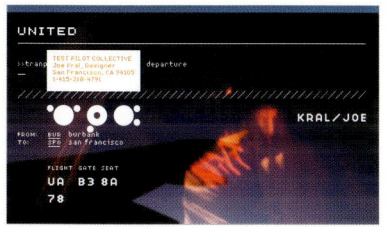

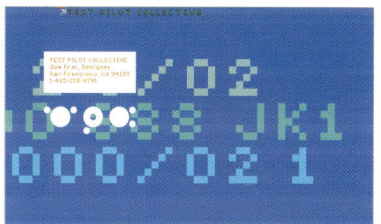

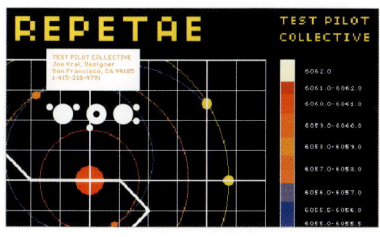

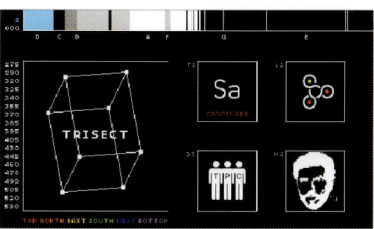

<u>Design/illustration</u>
Peepshow

<u>For</u>
Peepshow_
Illustration
collective_
London, UK

<u>Info</u>
This collective of illustrators use their cards to showcase
favourite work.

Sticky
PEEPSHOW

ILLUSTRATION COLLECTIVE
www.peepshow.org.uk

Design/illustration
Sean Alexander

For
Sean Alexander_
Designer_
London, UK

Info
An artist and designer, known for his unusual technique of
collaging vinyl on to board, Sean features details from his work
in this constantly evolving series of cards.

sean alexander

great western studios
great western road
london w9 3ny

studio 0207 289 8008
mail sean@laughingboy.tv
www.synergyart.co.uk

Design
 Mike Dorrian
Illustration
 Phil Ashcroft

For
 Phlash_
 Artist/illustrator_
 London, UK

Info
Phlash's cards showcase his obsessions in lurid techno-colour:
seventies sci-fi – Dr Who and Blake's 7– Star Wars, Bladerunner,
Dawn of the Dead, Godzilla, Ray Harryhausen's monsters, monsters
in general, Japanese toys and toxic landscapes.

PHLASH

Ground Floor Flat_
34 Waller Road_
London SE14 5LA_
0771 447 5029_
+44 (0)20 7639 5799_
e. philashcroft@hotmail.com
www.phlashweb.co.uk_

DJ SLACK
DEEJAY : PRODUCER : PROMOTER : PARTYROCKER!

JASON PLATTS
TERIYAKIANARKISAKI DIRECTOR

+ 61 (0) 412 544 769
SLACKMONSTER @ YAHOO.COM

WWW.TERIYAKIANARKISAKI.COM

<u>Design</u>
  Big Block Creative

<u>For</u>
  Teriyakianarkisaki_
  DJ/promoter_
  Melbourne,
  Australia

<u>Info</u>
  The philosophy at Big Block Creative is that business cards
  are in fact, "wallet-sized teenie weenie billboards for your
  personality". So shout it from the hilltop.

DOPEPOPE™
EXPERIMENTAL AESTHETICS:

Joe Gerardi: Mummenchanz

39W 14th St Suite 408 NYC 10011
P 212 206 7139 F 212 206 7138
www.dopepope.com

<u>Design</u>
DopePope
Joe Lucchese

<u>For</u>
DopePope_
Designer_
New York, USA

<u>Info</u>
A cast of invented sci-fi characters inhabit the DopePope
world and its stationery.

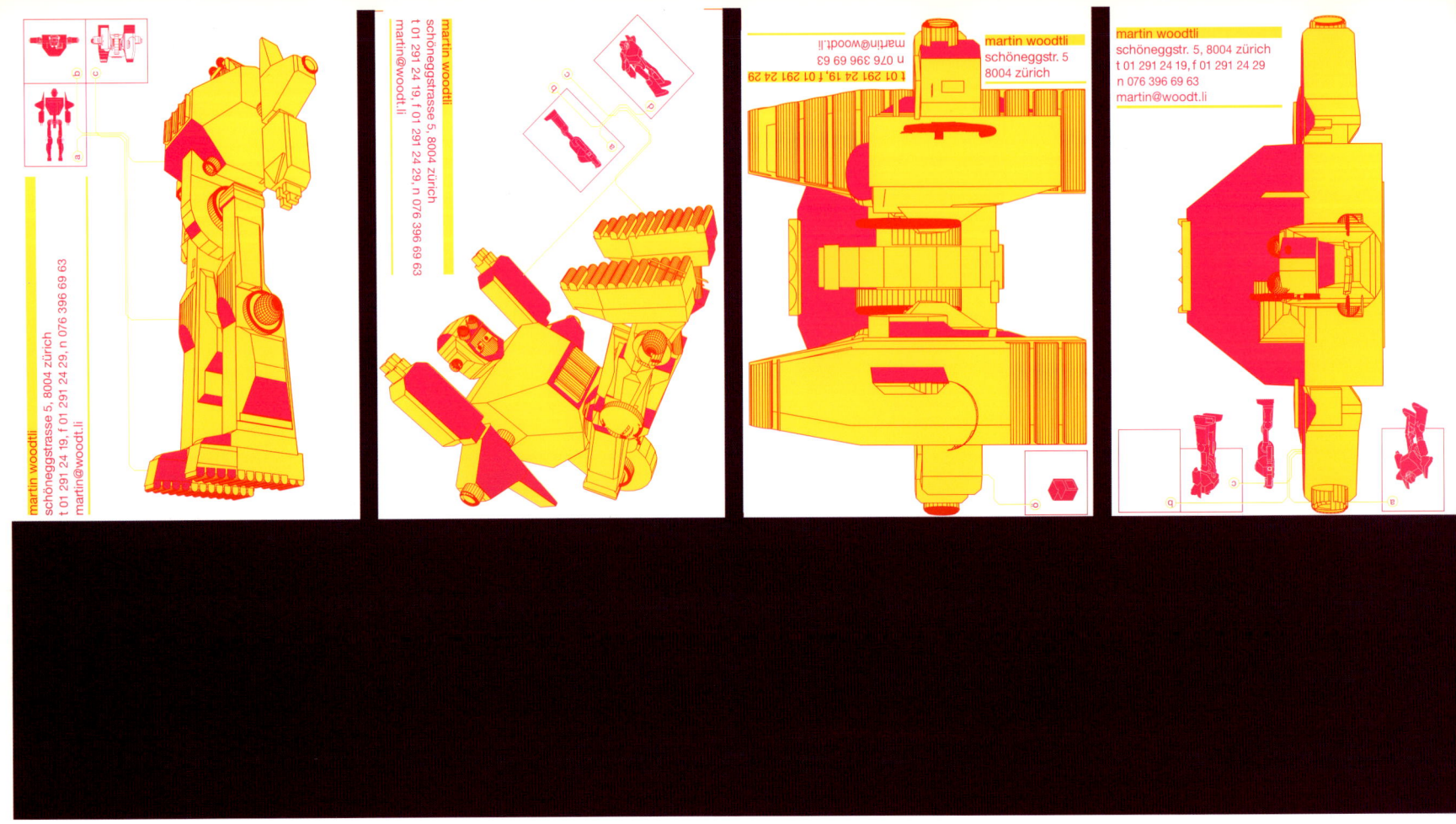

martin woodtli
schöneggstrasse 5, 8004 zürich
t 01 291 24 19, f 01 291 24 29, n 076 396 69 63
martin@woodt.li

martin woodtli
schöneggstrasse 5, 8004 zürich
t 01 291 24 19, f 01 291 24 29, n 076 396 69 63
martin@woodt.li

martin woodtli
schöneggstr. 5
8004 zürich
t 01 291 24 19, f 01 291 24 29
n 076 396 69 63
martin@woodt.li

martin woodtli
schöneggstr. 5, 8004 zürich
t 01 291 24 19, f 01 291 24 29
n 076 396 69 63
martin@woodt.li

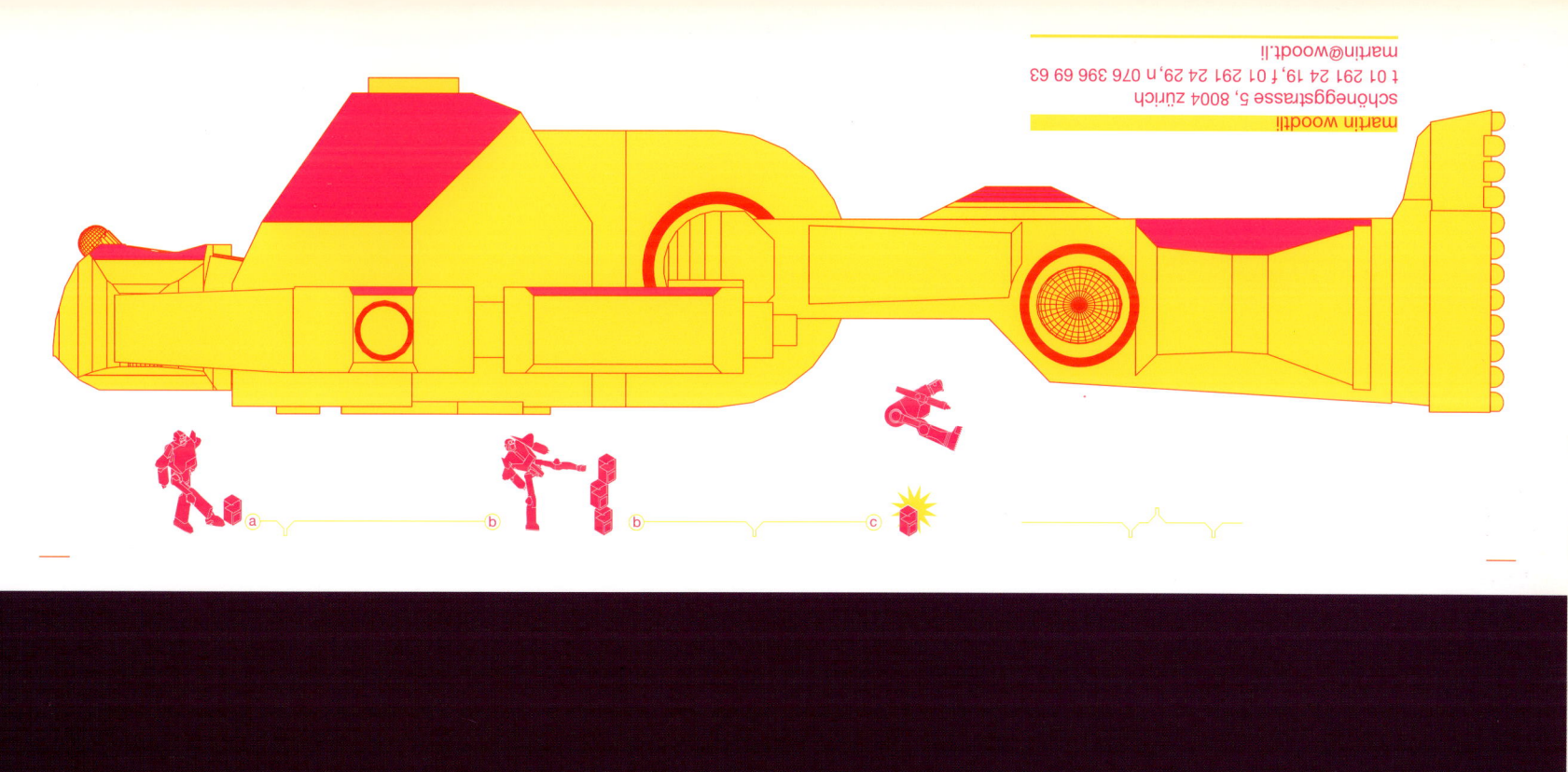

martin woodtli
schöneggstrasse 5, 8004 zürich
t 01 291 24 19, f 01 291 24 29, n 076 396 69 63
martin@woodt.li

Design
Martin Woodtli

For
Martin Woodtli_
Designer_
Zurich, Switzerland

Info
A lover of all things robotic, this series of cards includes handy hints on keeping your robot healthy. Contact details are buried within the copy. Highly visible and fun, these cards are cherished.

Design
Martin Woodtli

For
Katharina Lütscher_
Sports photographer_
Zurich, Switzerland

Info
Toy race-track components become business cards
when pressed out of this "model-making" sheet.

NICHOLAS BASTIN
1ka moar st fitzroy
australia 3065
tel 613 9417 4185

NICHOLAS BASTIN
tel 613 9417 4185

NICHOLAS BASTIN
tel 613 9417 4185

NICHOLAS BASTIN
tel 613 9417 4185

Design
Clear
Matthew McCarthy

For
Nicholas Bastin_
Jewellery designer_
Melbourne,
Australia

Info
A collage of objects collected by this jeweller was photographed and spread across a set of four perforated cards; complete, they act as a compliment slip.

123

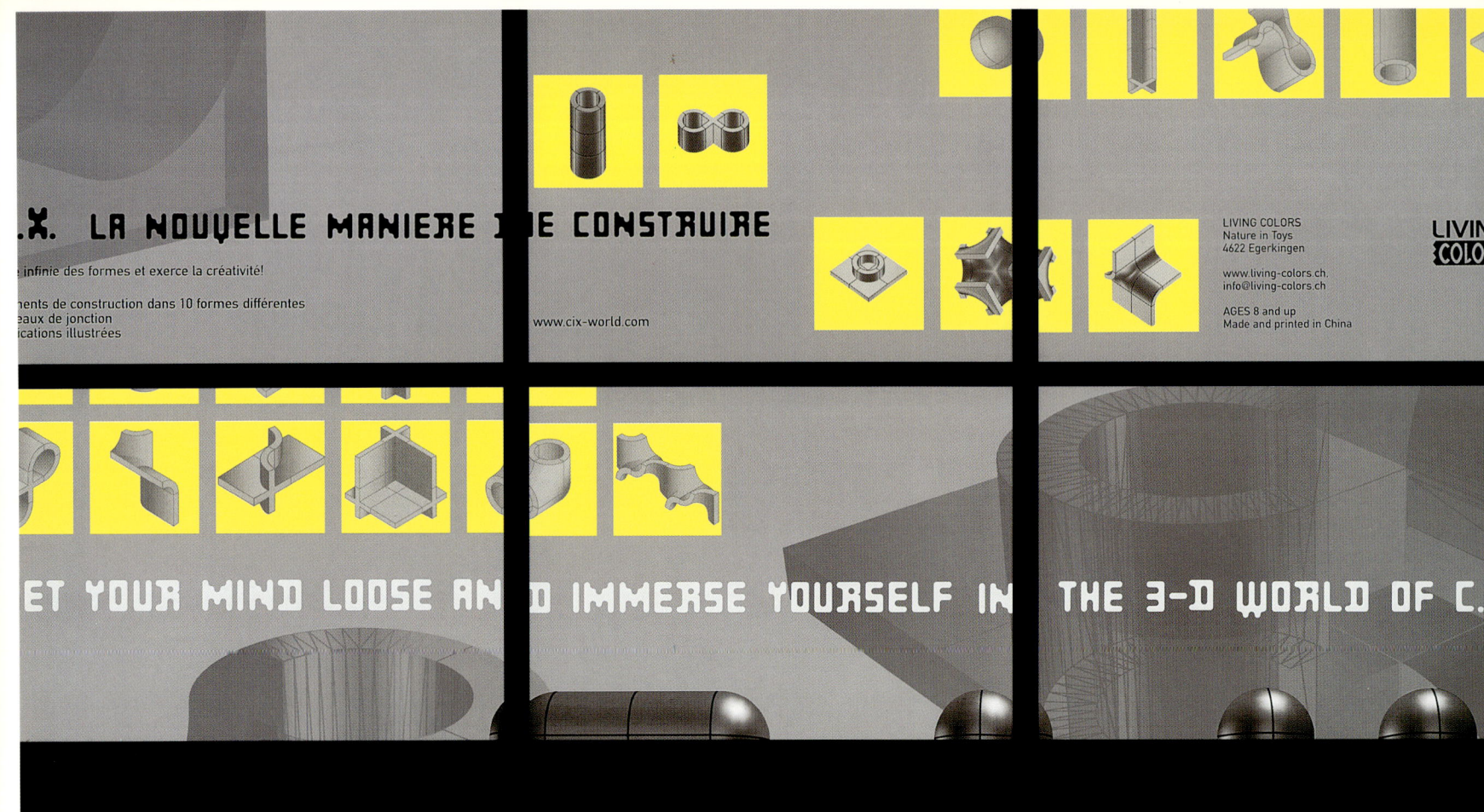

Design
Moxi

For
Living Colors_
Toy makers_
Egerkingen,
Switzerland

Info
This set of ten A6 cards for Living Colors fits together, just like
the C.I.X. construction puzzle they manufacture. One of them
is the business card.

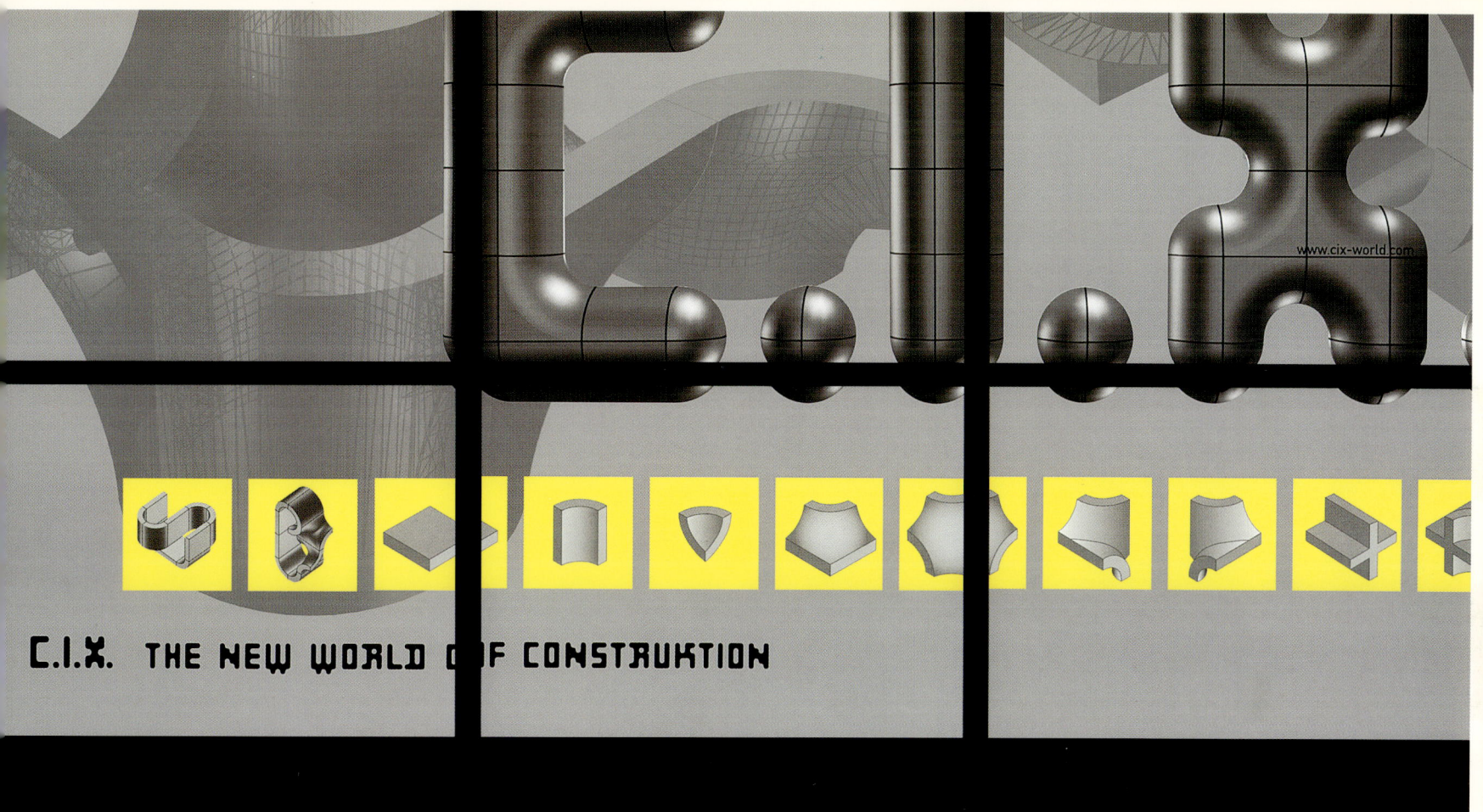

www.cix-world.com

C.I.X. THE NEW WORLD OF CONSTRUKTION

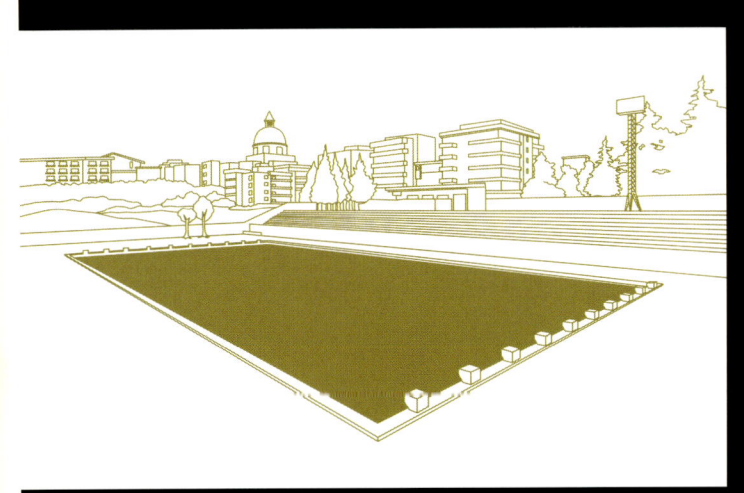

SHINOBU FUKUDA FOR HUGH

#403 4-16-28 SHIBOKU-HONCHO MIYAMAE-KU KAWASAKI-SHI KANAGAWA PREF. 216-0031 JAPAN
TEL +81-44-829-0851 FAX +81-44-829-0850   EMAIL FUKU-S@INTERLINK.OR.JP

Design
HUGH

For
HUGH_
Designers_
Kanagawa,
Japan

Info
Each partner in this design duo has both versions of the business card. Depicted in white ink on gold stock, the mirror images signify that two personalities may work as a unit.

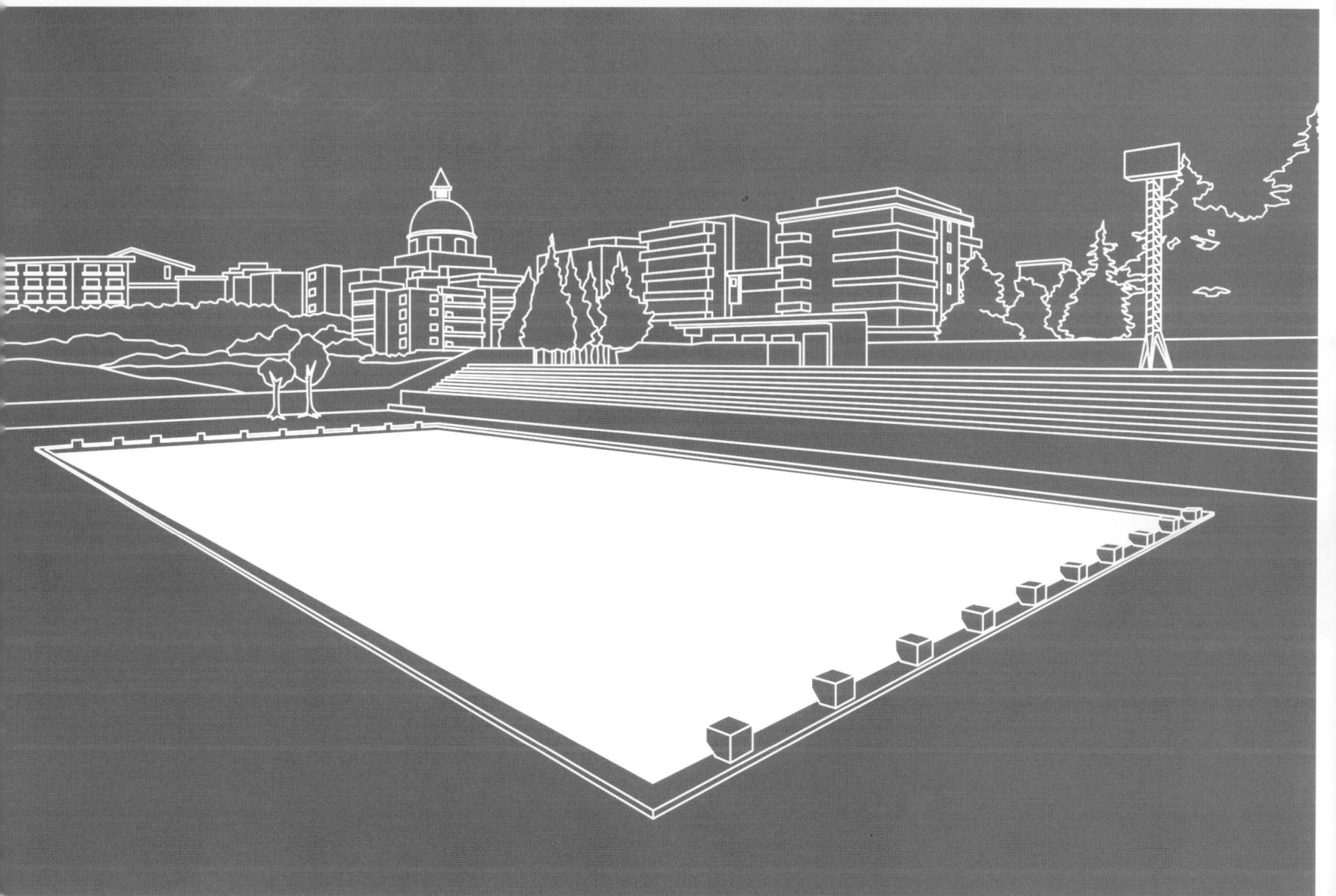

MMM@DIGITALMASTURBATION.COM
PO BOX 1729 NEW FARM Q 4005 **AUSTRALIA**
MB +61 418 876 232 FX +617 3358 3738

Design
Rinzen

For
Digital Masturbation_
Experimental musicians_
New Farm, Australia

Info
Exploiting the viscose quality of UV varnish, the drips and
splashes on this card refer to the metaphorical outcome of
self-indulgent noodling by digital artists and musicians.
They've obviously got a sense of humour.

PROVIDING COMMUNICATION THROUGH GRAPHICS

3 6 0

Plazma

Todd Hansson >>> Designer

Plazma Group >>> 4.15 Woodcock St >>> Paddington >>> Q >>> Australia
T/F +61 7 3369 6353 >>> M 0401 134 626 >>> E plazma@gil.com.au

Plazma

Design
 Plazma
 Todd Hansson

For
 Plazma_
 Designers_
 Sydney, Australia

Info
 Type and illustrative elements merge and jumble in a
 disorienting void; on the reverse, though, Plazma's contact
 details are tightly ordered.

 **Iyengar Yoga
classes**

Elizabeth
Smullens

Reichenbergerstrasse 149
10999 Berlin · Germany

+49 30 61 62 66 76
+49 173 626 76 40
greenshoot@hotmail.com
www.elizabethsmullens.com

**performance · dance ·
video projects**

Elizabeth
Smullens

Reichenbergerstrasse 149
10999 Berlin · Germany

+49 30 61 62 66 76
+49 173 626 76 40
greenshoot@hotmail.com
www.elizabethsmullens.com

Design
  Büro Ludwig

For
  Elizabeth Smullens_
  Performance artist/
  yoga teacher_
  Berlin, Germany

Info
  Sometime performance artist and part-time yoga teacher
  Elizabeth tears these double-sided, perforated cards in half,
  so as to hand over appropriate details for whichever situation.

craig metzger
enginesystem.com
craig@enginesystem.com | 718.812.9273

Design
Enginesystem
Craig Metzger

For
Enginesystem_
Designer_
New York, USA

Info
To be untypical, Craig rounded the corners of his card, chose
bright colours ("I'd never seen a magenta business card before"),
and decided to highlight his image-making over information
("which I know is totally wrong"). And why not?

RINZEN.COM

<u>Design</u>
Rinzen

<u>For</u>
Rinzen_
Designers_
Australia

<u>Info</u>
Each studio member has a signature balloon; the web address completes the card as frequent studio moves make printed addresses obsolete. These multi-functional cards spread the word as business cards, swing tags on Rinzen products, and flyers at shows and exhibitions.

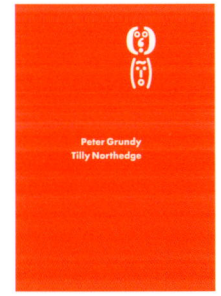

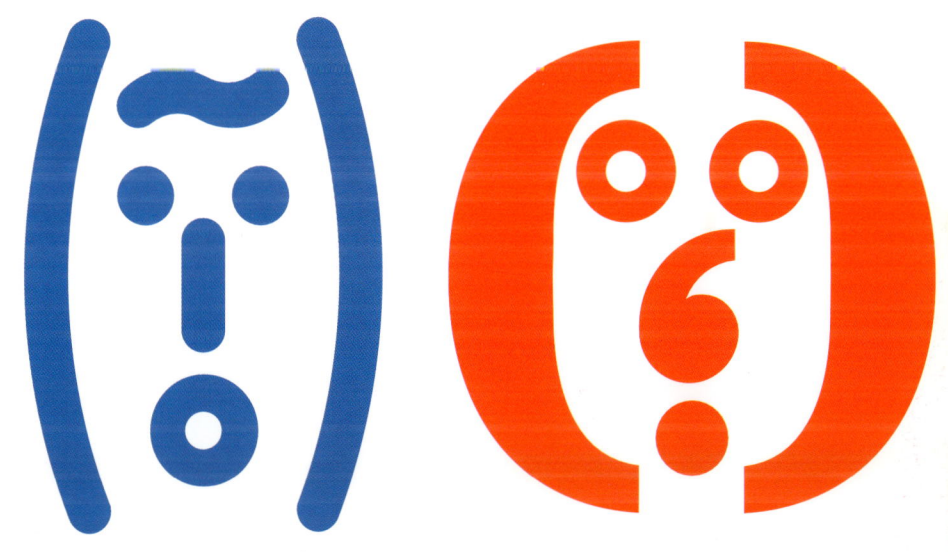

Peter Grundy
Tilly Northedge

Telephone :
+44 (0)20 8995 2452

Fax :
+44 (0)20 8995 3049

Email :
all@grundynorthedge.com

Website :
www.grundynorthedge.com

<u>Design</u>
Grundy & Northedge
Peter Grundy_
Tilly Northedge

<u>For</u>
Grundy & Northedge_
Information designers_
London, UK

<u>Info</u>
Renowned designers of information graphics, this partnership present themselves as "pure information", albeit with a sense of humour.

MATT PATTINSON
M - 0781 641 3521
E - mattpatt.520@virgin.net
W - www.culprit-art.com

CULPRIT

Design/illustration
 Culprit-art
 Matt Pattinson

For
 Culprit-art_
 Designer/illustrator_
 London, UK

Info
 Matt creates characters using a distinctive combination of black
 line and flat colour. His cards are a portable gallery; some are
 also stickers.

<u>Design/photography</u>
Burncrew

<u>For</u>
Burncrew_
Designers/
clothing label
Melbourne,
Australia

<u>Info</u>
This Melbourne-based collective of artists, designers and graffiti-
writers produces work in a range of media and at various scales.
Their signature rioter, van and flame logo appear on t-shirts,
canvases and walls alike, and their technique of combining
stencil and Xerox is replicated on this set of cards.

Brendan Elliott
61 (0) 414 532 073
Burn Clothing
PO Box 393 Clifton Hill
VIC 3068 Australia

Tel/Fax: 61 (3) 9482 2655
Email: brendan@burncrew.com   www.burncrew.com

space3eindhoven > postbus 8007, 5601 KA Eindhoven
T 040 213 53 67 > F 040 213 53 75 > E space3@ooo.nl

Design
 Space3

For
 Space3_
 Designers_
 Eindhoven,
 The Netherlands

Info
 These artists/designers/illustrators are as at home altering urban
 environments with sticker and poster campaigns as they are
 working commercially; consequently their card has a "cool"
 information side (with a space for stickers), and an anarchic
 reverse featuring various characters and slogans.

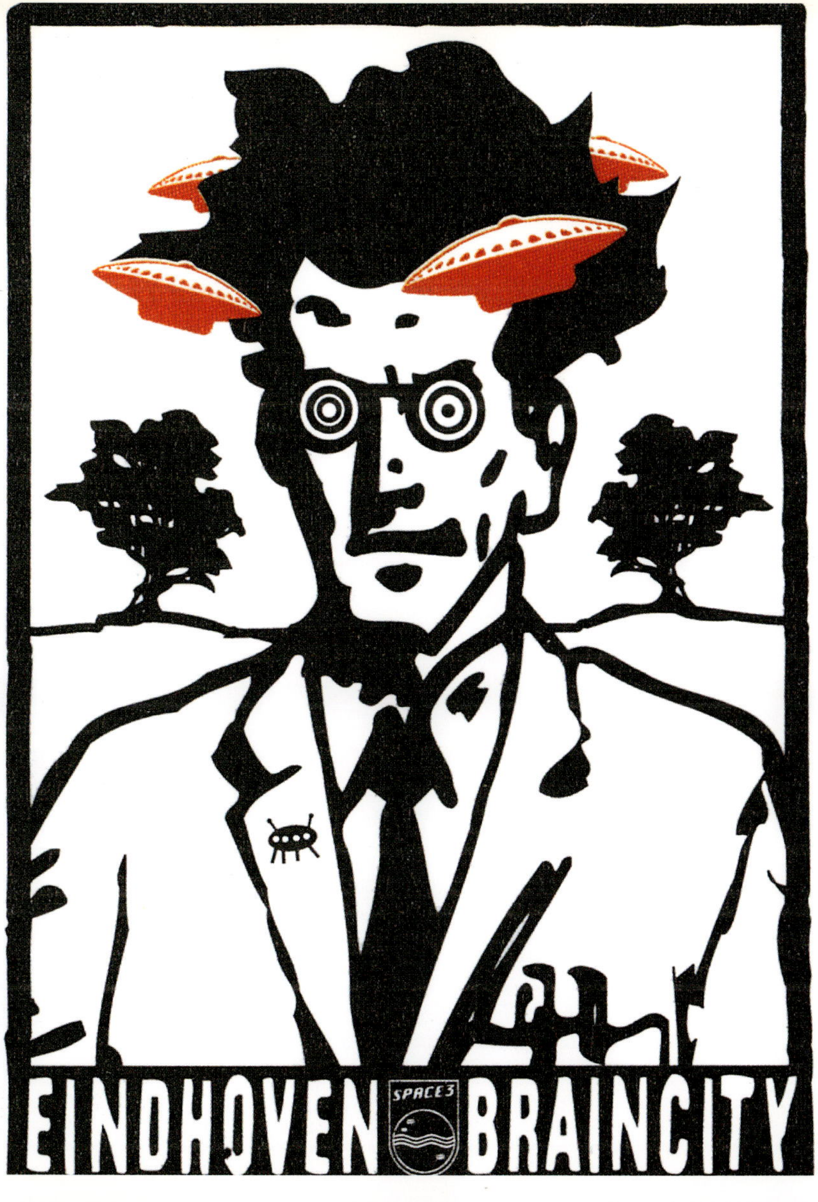
EINDHOVEN
SPACE3
BRAINCITY

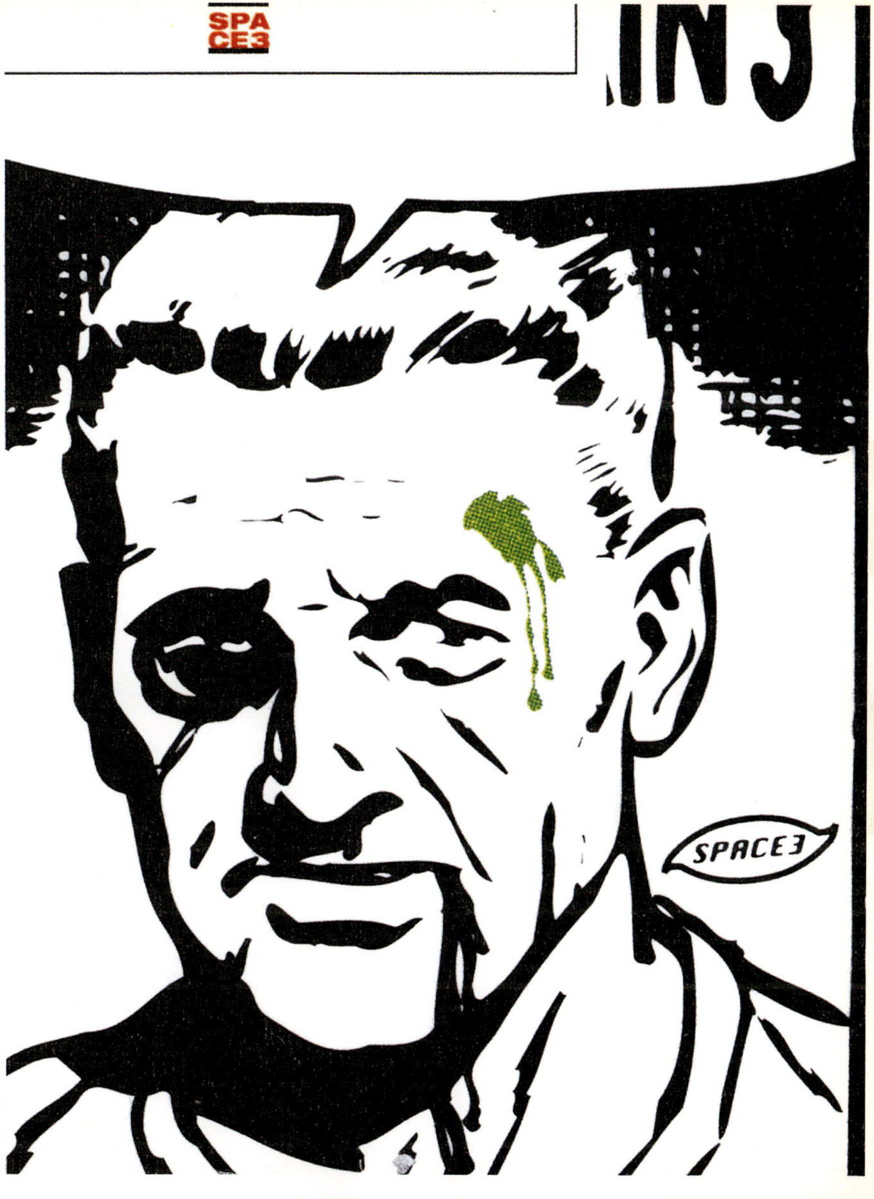
SPA
CE3
SPACE3

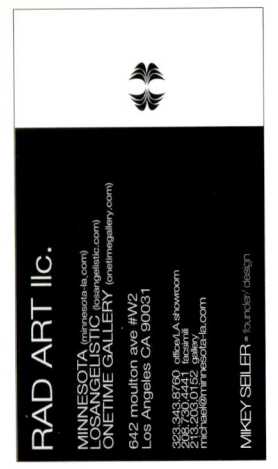

RAD ART llc.

MINNESOTA (minnesota-la.com)
LOS ANGELES LLC (losangelistic.com)
ONETIME GALLERY (onetimegallery.com)

642 moulton ave #W2
Los Angeles CA 90031

323.343.8760   office/LA showroom
208.730.4441   facsimili
213.200.0152   gallery
michael@minnesota-la.com

MIKEY SEILER ° founder/design

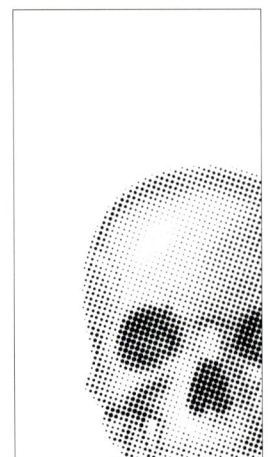

quickdraw.

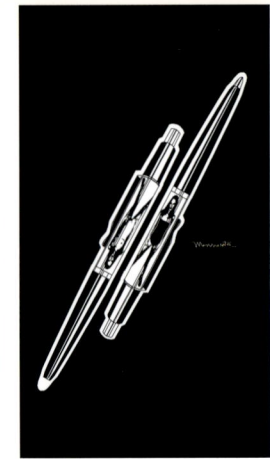

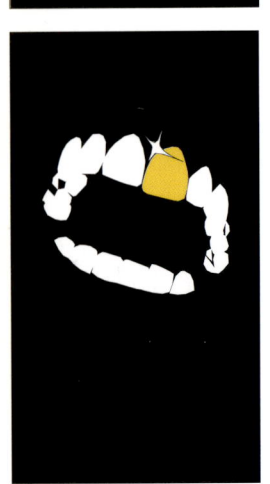

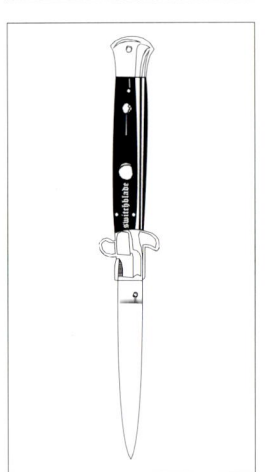

Design
Rad Art llc
Mikey Seiler

For
Rad Art llc_
Designer/gallery/
clothing label_
Los Angeles, USA

Info
An art-factory, Minnesota is home to a design studio, a clothing
and homewares label and a street-art gallery. That wide range
of activity is reflected in the myriad imagery, featuring urban
and pop-culture icons, found on these cards.

140

ALUMNI
skateboarding

★

FAVORITE TRICK:
GETTING THE GUYS
TO LISTEN
Deanna takes care of all the Alumni
stuff the guys are scared to do.

DEANNA WAGGONER
TREASURER
deanna@alumniskateboarding.com

2812426555

★

FAVORITE TRICK:
BONELESS
Art is an aspiring carpenter.
He has built numerous skateparks
in the Houston area.

ART WAGGONER
PRESIDENT
art@alumniskateboarding.com

2812426555

★

FAVORITE TRICK:
TAKE A KID SKATING
Give us a call if you have any questions

NOT OLD SCHOOL, NOT NEW SCHOOL
THE SCHOOL
theschool@alumniskateboarding.com

2812426555

Design
J6 Studios
Tim Jester

For
Alumni_
Skateboard
company_
Houston, USA

Info
For this skateboard label aimed at the over-thirties, the focus is on
having fun, passing skills on to the kids, and generally being
old-skool. The card's shape evolved from its origin as a swing tag.

142

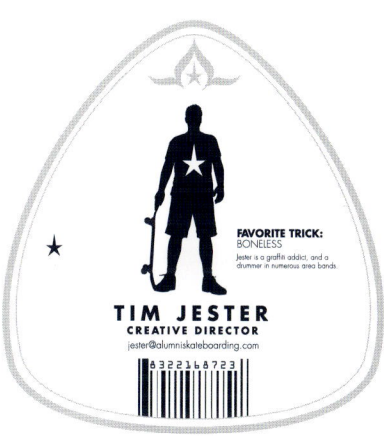

FAVORITE TRICK:
BONELESS
Jester is a graffiti addict, and a drummer in numerous area bands.

TIM JESTER
CREATIVE DIRECTOR
jester@alumniskateboarding.com

4322168723

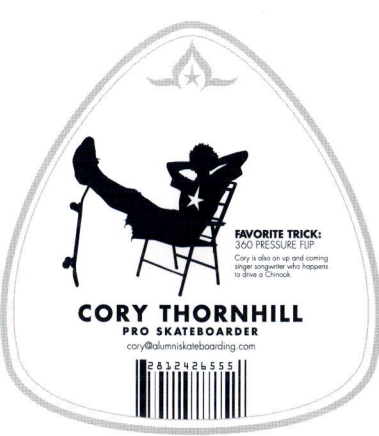

FAVORITE TRICK:
360 PRESSURE FLIP
Cory is also an up and coming singer songwriter who happens to drive a Chinook.

CORY THORNHILL
PRO SKATEBOARDER
cory@alumniskateboarding.com

2812426555

FAVORITE TRICK:
360 PRESSURE FLIP
Cory is also an up and coming singer songwriter who happens to drive a Chinook.

CORY THORNHILL
PRO SKATEBOARDER
cory@alumniskateboarding.com

2812426555

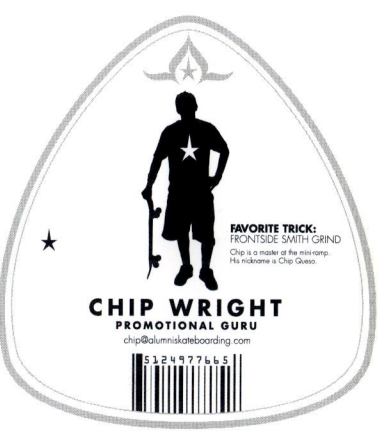

FAVORITE TRICK:
FRONTSIDE SMITH GRIND
Chip is a master at the mini-ramp. His nickname is Chip Queso.

CHIP WRIGHT
PROMOTIONAL GURU
chip@alumniskateboarding.com

5124977665

Design/illustration
Jorge Alderete

For
Nicotyna_
Rockabilly band_
Mexico City,
Mexico

Info
Jorge created a classic rock'n'roll icon for this Mexican rockabilly band, combining elements of tattoo designs, pin-ups and hot-rod art.

Laura Delgado
Suscripciones

Raúl Guillén Bernáldez
Administrador General

Silvia Guillén
Director

complot

Editorial Guillén Mexicana S.A. de C.V.
Vermont # 34 - 6
Col. Nápoles (03810), México, D.F.
Tels-Fax: 5543-3341 / 5543-8097
e-mail: guillen@complot1.com

Clarisa Moura
Director de Arte

Rodrigo de Alba
Coordinador Editorial

Norma Lazo
Editor

Design
 Clarisa Moura
Illustration
 Jorge Alderete

For
 Complot_
 Magazine_
 Mexico City,
 Mexico

Info
 Sophisticated mid-century modern cartoons of staff members
 accentuate the aesthetic of this lifestyle journal.

Design/illustration
laVista_
Patrick Thomas

For
laVista_
Designers_
Barcelona, Spain

Info
A set of black, red and white images, these cards may
be a cryptic puzzle; they are also a mini portfolio of recent
illustrations.

<u>Design</u>
Airside

<u>For</u>
Airside_
Designers_
London, UK

<u>Info</u>
Colourful portraits in a signature style grace Airside's cards,
highlighting the individuals who make up this multi-disciplinary
design company.

airside

alex maclean
director
alex@airside.co.uk
24 cross street
london n1 2bg
tel: +44 (0)20 7354 9912
fax: +44 (0)20 7354 5529
www.airside.co.uk

Design
Pfadfinderei

For
BPitch Control_
Record label_
Berlin, Germany

Info
Wildly differing imagery is framed within a template that lets
you know which way is up; type relates to the diagonal of the
cut-off corner, thus becoming part of the image rather than simply
being placed on top. The illustrations and photos represent artists
and releases from this record label.

you

are beauti-
ful

kerry roper designer+illustrator

t. +44 (0)7976 774820

www.youarebeautiful.co.uk

Design
You Are Beautiful
Kerry Roper

For
You Are Beautiful_
Designer/illustrator_
London, UK

Info
A typographer and designer, Kerry demonstrates her all-round
versatility with this series of cards; she took the photos too.
Everyone's beautiful in their own unique way.

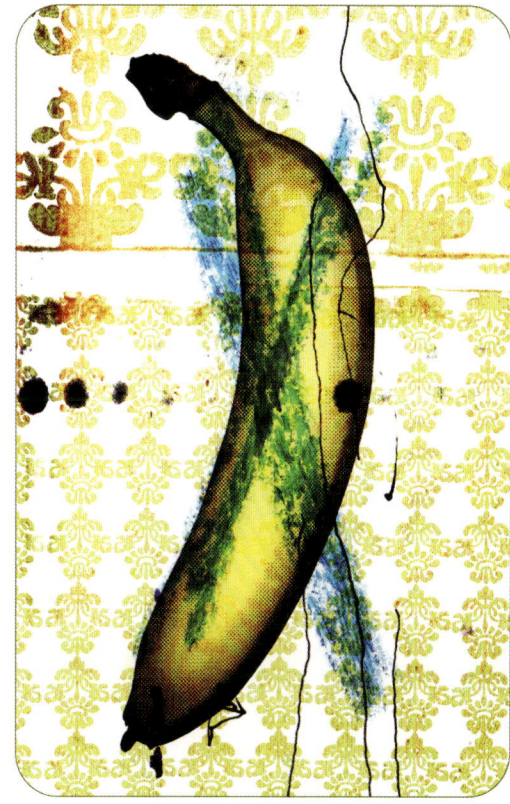

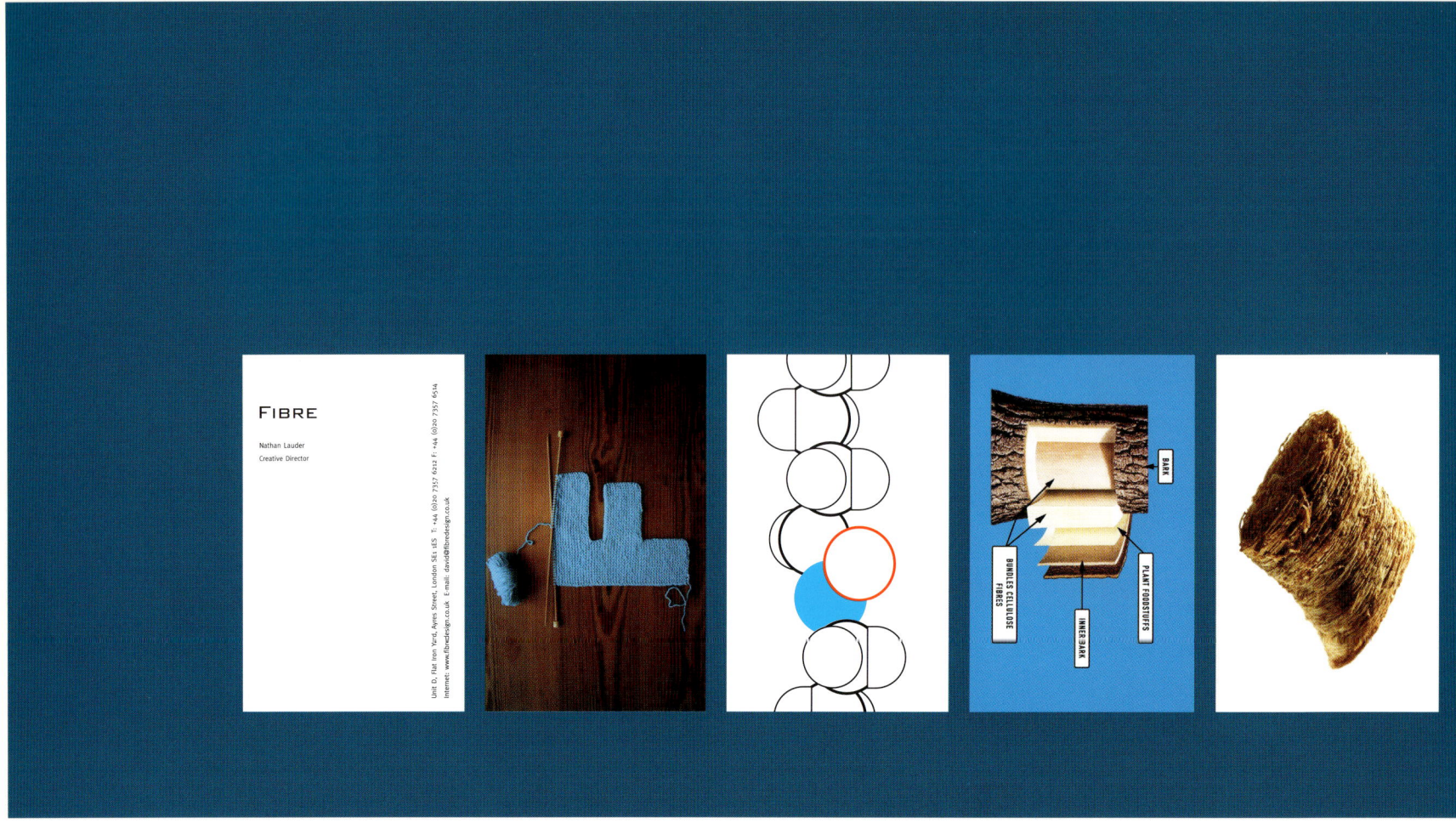

FIBRE

Nathan Lauder
Creative Director

Unit D, Flat Iron Yard, Ayres Street, London SE1 1ES T: +44 (0)20 7357 6212 F: +44 (0)20 7357 6514
Internet: www.fibredesign.co.uk E-mail: david@fibredesign.co.uk

BARK

BUNDLES CELLULOSE FIBRES

PLANT FOODSTUFFS

INNER BARK

Design
Fibre
Nathan Lauder_
Tommy Miller_
David Rainbird_
Hannah Titterington

For
Fibre_
Designers_
London, UK

Info
Communicating the breadth of their multiple-media expertise, Fibre
originated diverse imagery in various "languages" to be printed on
the reverse of all stationery items. A pack of twelve cards are sealed
in cereal-box-style polythene bags and used as mailers or "leave
behinds".

154

Glassfibre
Resin

RAINBIRD

SHRED THIS BUSINESS CARD

I ♥ NYLON

Design
  Big Block Creative

For
  Wankuss_
  Designers_
  Melbourne,
  Australia

Info
  A zine and t-shirt company for boys who like all things loud
  and gratuitous – hence the signature monster truck. This card
  welcomes you into their world!

Design
Big Block Creative

For
Nitrous Industries_
Designers_
Melbourne,
Australia

Info
Big, brash and Aussie: hot-rods and muscle cars are the
favoured cultural references. Ironic or not, you decide.

Strut
2 Hargrave Place
London
N7 0BP

Telephone
+44 (0)20 7485 7855
Facsimile
+44 (0)20 7284 1151

Internet
www.strut.co.uk

Toni Rossano

Email
toni.rossano@strut.co.uk
Mobile phone
+44 (0)7958 474 564

Tinku Bhattacharyya

Email
tinku@strut.co.uk
Mobile phone
+44 (0)7968 176 391

Design
  Amp Associates

For
  Strut_
  Record label_
  London, UK

Info
  Photography rendered in bold silhouette evokes
  aesthetic and lifestyle choices.

Design/photography
CHK Design
Christian Küsters

For
Boyarsky Murphy_
Architects_
London, UK

Info
Aware of the architects' concern with surface, texture and
process, Christian chose three details from an image of an
urban space, and zoomed in to exaggerate the print process
into pattern. This series of cards is a taster that may draw the
viewer further into their work.

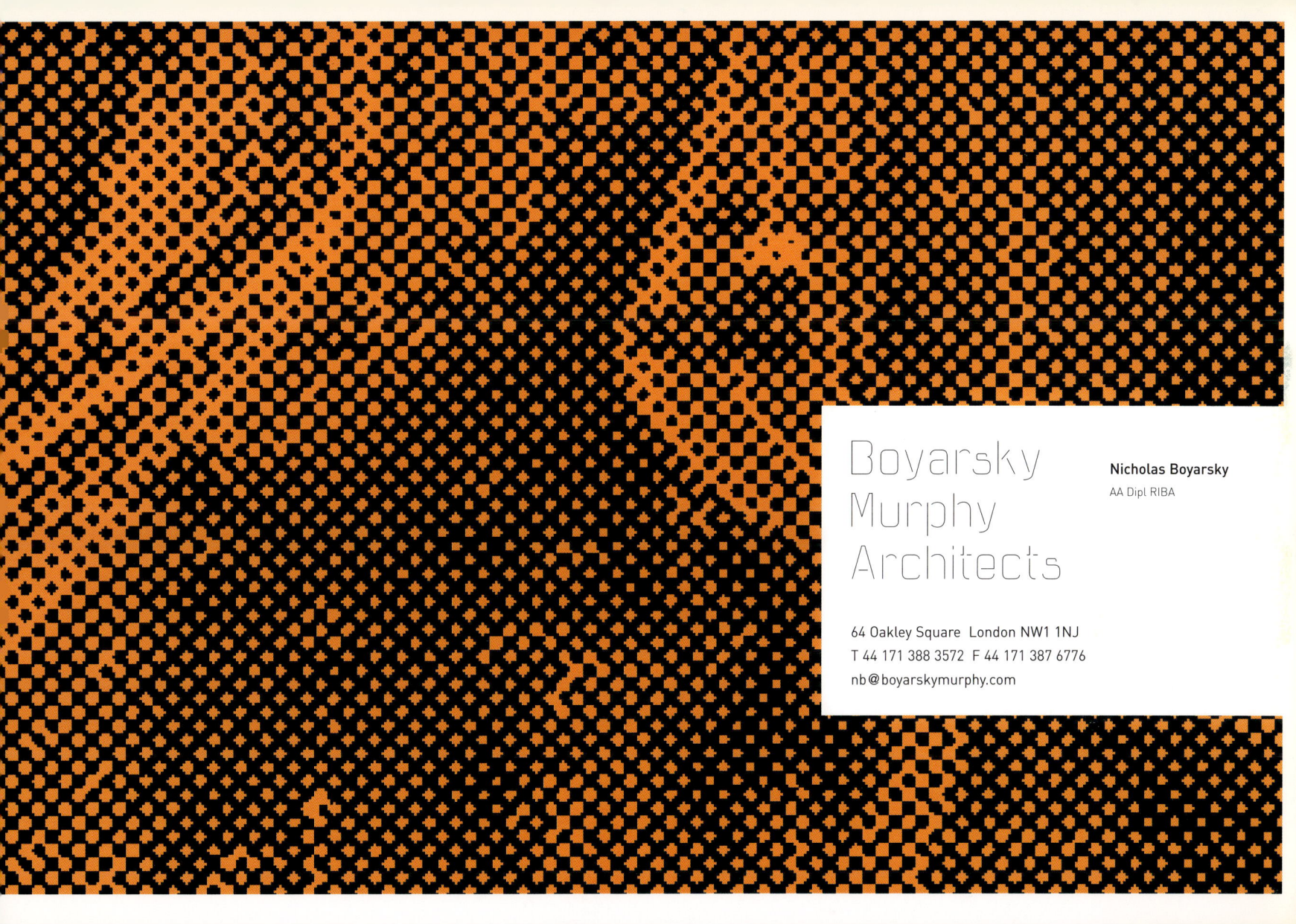

Boyarsky
Murphy
Architects

Nicholas Boyarsky

AA Dipl RIBA

64 Oakley Square London NW1 1NJ
T 44 171 388 3572 F 44 171 387 6776
nb@boyarskymurphy.com

ALARICHSTR_18_A 70469_STUTTGART

service:
Marcus_Fischer

№
0711_85_10_80

ALARICHSTR.18A 70496 STGT

DISCODOENER

service:
MARCUS_FISCHER
PIT_LEDERLE

№
0711_85_10_80

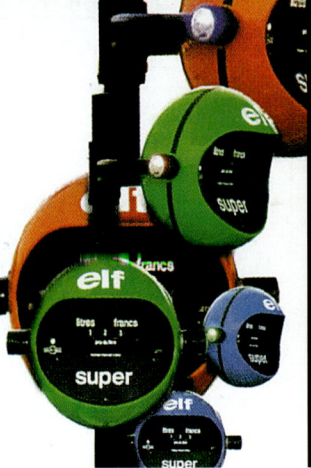

service:
ALARICHSTR_18_A
70469_STUTTGART

PIT_LEDERLE

№
0711_85_10_80

Design
 Discodoener
 Marcus Fischer_
 Pit Lederle

For
 Discodoener
 Designers_
 Stuttgart, Germany

Info
 Celebrating speed and consumerism; with typography
 reminiscent of till receipts, matched to imagery glorifying
 car culture.

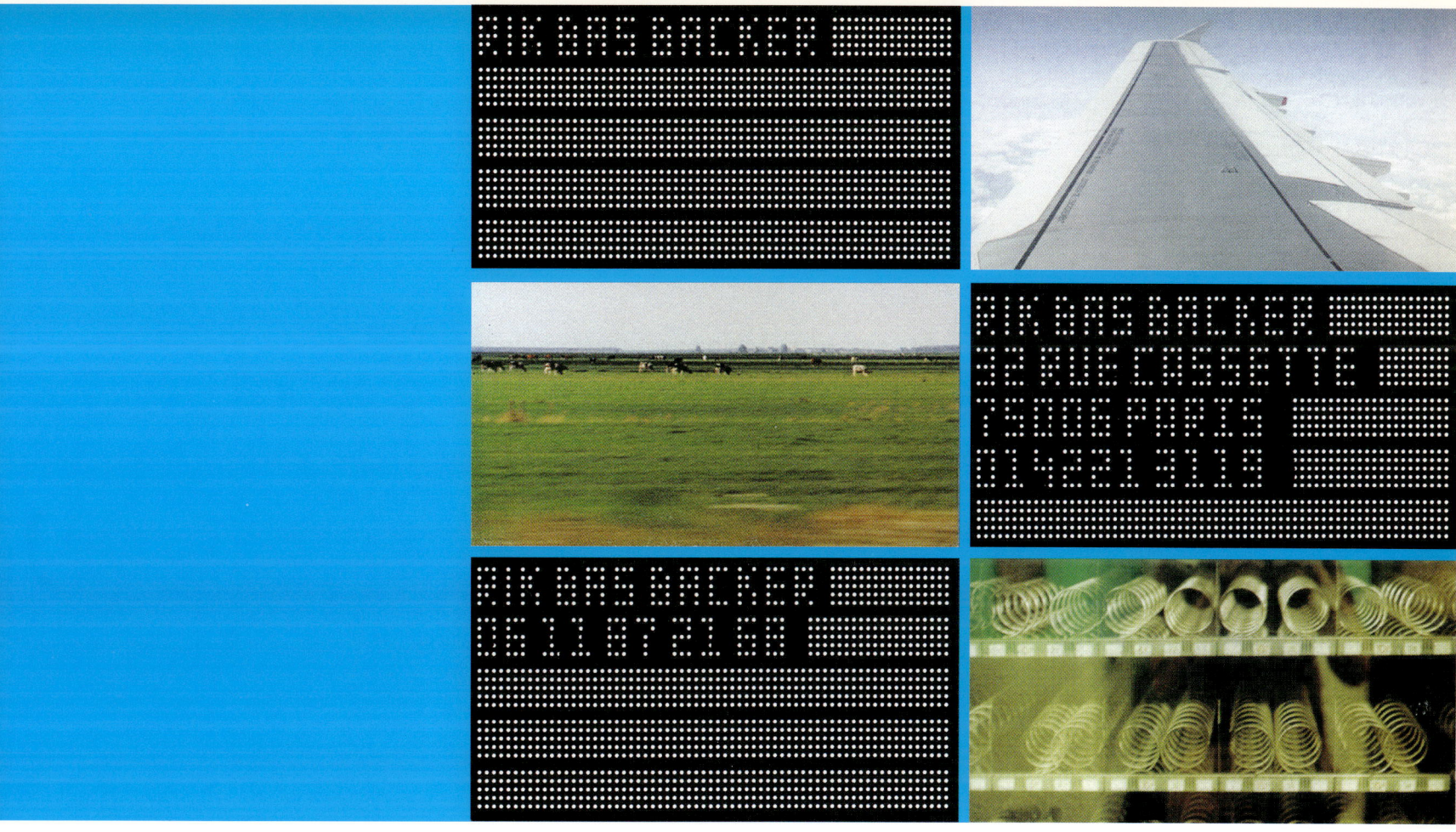

<u>Design/photography</u>
Rik Bas Backer

<u>For</u>
Rik Bas Backer_
Photographer_
Paris, France

<u>Info</u>
With a black pen, the matrix of white dots on Rik's card may
be customized to spell out his ever-changing contact details.
The idea was inspired by the giant price tags at petrol stations.

#04 ARROWS

#17 BEING HAPPY

#32 COOPER BLACK

<u>Design/photography</u>
Carl Ison

<u>For</u>
Carl Ison_
Designer/
photographer_
London, UK

<u>Info</u>
Entitled "Things that inspire me", the thematic connectedness
of these cards is stressed by their concertina, perforated format,
and the way each image slips into the next.

DRAUGHT ASSOCIATES LIMITED
WWW.DRAUGHT.CO.UK

MICHAEL LENZ
MICHAEL@DRAUGHT.CO.UK

133 Curtain Road
London EC2A 3BX
T 020 7739 3210
F 020 7739 3304
M 07957 688 250

Design/photography
Draught Associates
Dave Gibson_
Michael Lenz

For
Draught Associates_
Designers_
London, UK

Info
As part of an identity that runs across stationery, portfolios and sketchbooks, Draught select snapshots, research and reference photos from inspirational material used on previous projects. The aim is to provide insight into their working method without relating to specific jobs.

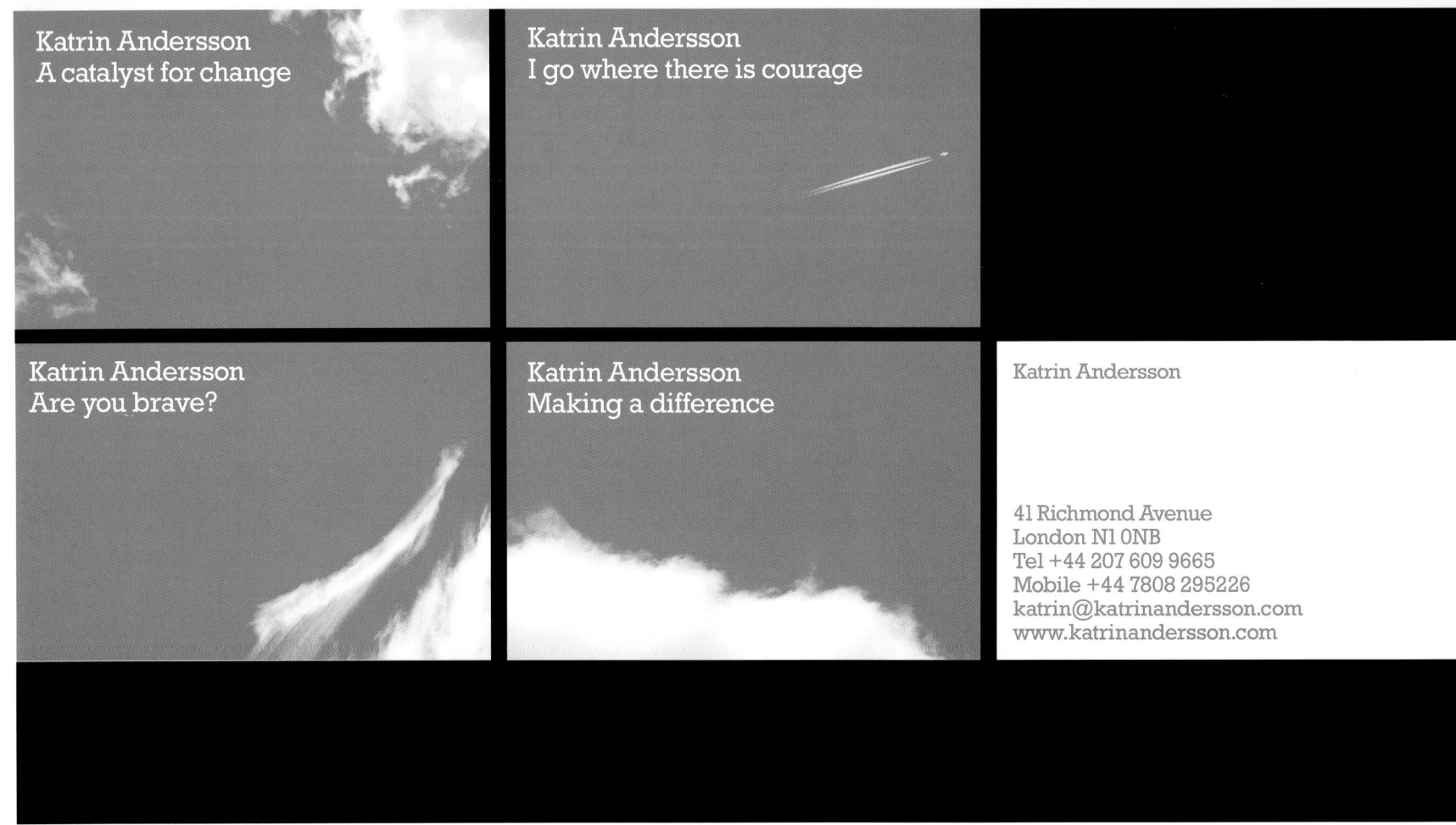

Katrin Andersson
A catalyst for change

Katrin Andersson
I go where there is courage

Katrin Andersson
Are you brave?

Katrin Andersson
Making a difference

Katrin Andersson

41 Richmond Avenue
London N1 0NB
Tel +44 207 609 9665
Mobile +44 7808 295226
katrin@katrinandersson.com
www.katrinandersson.com

Design
 CDT Design
 Nevs Hamling

For
 Katrin Andersson_
 Consultant_
 London, UK

Info
 Blue-sky thinking and new perspectives are the metaphors
 at work for this business consultant who specializes in enabling
 change and unlocking potential.

Design/photography
Monica Pirovano

For
Monica Pirovano_
Designer_
London, UK

Info
Monica combines her own photography with bold silver-foil
blocked type; depending on the light, you read text or image.

Design/photography | For | Info
Influenza | Influenza_ Artist/designer_ Rotterdam, The Netherlands | These business cards "without a business address" are from an illustrator/designer/street artist. He aims for them to work on many levels; as visual aids during talks and performances, as documentation of his activities and as collectibles.

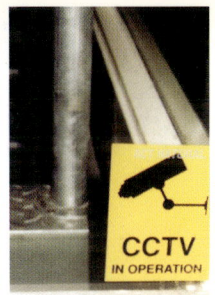
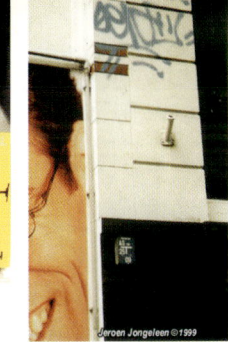

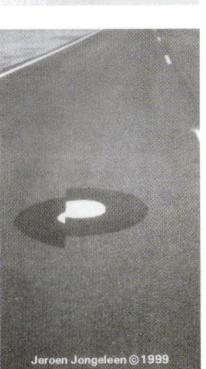
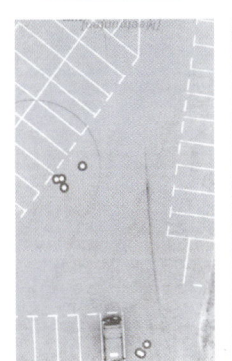

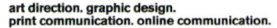

art direction. graphic design.
print communication. online communication.

Büro Ludwig

Birte Ludwig
www.buero-ludwig.com
info@buero-ludwig.com

+49 177 727 48 54

art direction. graphic design.
print communication. online communication.

Büro Ludwig

Birte Ludwig
www.buero-ludwig.com
info@buero-ludwig.com

+49 177 727 48 54

art direction. graphic design.
print communication. online communication.

Büro Ludwig

Birte Ludwig
www.buero-ludwig.com
info@buero-ludwig.com

+49 177 727 48 54

art direction. graphic design.
print communication. online communication.

Büro Ludwig

Birte Ludwig
www.buero-ludwig.com
info@buero-ludwig.com

+49 177 727 48 54

art direction. graphic design.
print communication. online communication.

Büro Ludwig

Birte Ludwig
www.buero-ludwig.com
info@buero-ludwig.com

+49 177 727 48 54

Design
Büro Ludwig
Birte Ludwig

For
Büro Ludwig_
Designer_
Berlin, Germany

Info
In a space entitled "official work station", freelance Birte pastes tiny images of possible work environments cut from photos and postcards; the implication being that she'll bring design solutions to wherever they are needed.

J. VAN DIJK
COPYWRITER
STUURMANKADE 198 · 1019 WC · AMSTERDAM
TEL/FAX+31(0)20-4198148 · MOBILE+31(0)654-627482
E-MAIL JOB@XS4ALL·NL

<u>Design</u>
KesselsKramer

<u>For</u>
J. van Dijk_
Copywriter_
Amsterdam,
The Netherlands

<u>Info</u>
It being a common name in Holland, signs denoting other
"J. van Dijks" were appropriated for this copywriter's card.

173

Carol Grant
partner

Grant Riches
communication consultants

4 Borough Street
Brighton BN1 3BG
telephone 01273 233036
mobile 07711 819604
carol@grantriches.co.uk
www.grantriches.co.uk

<u>Design</u>
 The Team
<u>Photography</u>
 Andrew Hall

<u>For</u>
 Grant Riches_
 Communication
 consultants_
 London, UK

<u>Info</u>
Someone's name or an optimistic plea, Grant Riches are a
copywriting duo whose cards capture playful, atmospheric
and poignant observations from everyday life.

Design
Cake

For
Cake_
Creative
consultancy_
London, UK

Info
Mouth-watering images from "how to" cake-making
manuals demand to be lingered over; these cards
will never be thrown away!

cake

Creative Business

JAMES-LEE DUFFY

james@cakemedia.com

Cake, 10 Stephen Mews
London W1T 1AG
www.cakegroup.com

D (+44) 20 7307 3136
M 07791 717 791

T (+44) 20 7307 3100
F (+44) 20 7307 3101
Isdn (+44) 20 7436 8318

200 St John Street London EC1V 4RN
mother@motherlondon.com
T 020 7689 0689 F 020 7689 1689

proud mother of JESSICA LOVELL

proud mother of ALAN MOSELEY

proud mother of VICKY GHOSE

proud mother of THOMAS HILLAND

proud mother of SOPHIE SPENCE

proud mother of LUKE WILLIAMSON

proud mother of ANNA BIRD

proud mother of ANDY BELLASS

proud mother of SARAH COATES

Design
Mother
Luke Williamson

For
Mother_
Advertising
agency_
London, UK

Info
True to their name and their wacky image, this ad agency's
cards feature a collection of stunning, cute and wild (by turns)
photos of the staffers' mothers. On the reverse are lurid wallpaper
patterns, denoting the vintage era favoured by Mother's interior
decorators.

proud mother of JOE DE SOUZA

proud mother of KERRY MILLETT

proud mother of SEBASTIAN WILHELM

proud mother of NATALIE PHELAN

proud mother of AL MACCUISH

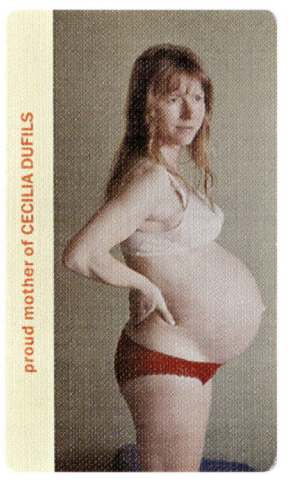

proud mother of CECILIA DUFILS

proud mother of CHARLIE JOHNSON

proud mother of CAROLINE PAY

proud mother of WILL McMULLAN

proud mother of KIM GEHRIG

proud mother of ANDY MEDD

proud mother of GEORGINA BURDEN

proud mother of LAURENCE THOMSON

proud mother of ZOE BELL

proud mother of JUAN CABRAL

proud mother of SAM FERGUSON

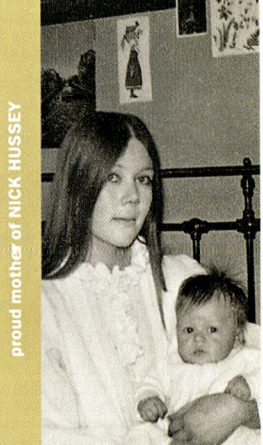

proud mother of NICK HUSSEY

proud mother of ZUZA KOVAC

proud mother of JANINE LEVY

proud mother of MALIN WIKERBERG

180

proud mother of MARK WHELAN

proud mother of TAMMY BLACKMORE

proud mother of IAIN NEWTON

proud mother of CATHERINE NICKSON

proud mother of SAM WALKER

proud mother of CHERISE THOMSON

proud mother of STEF CALCRAFT

proud mother of DEBBIE LONGMUIR

proud mother of YAN ELLIOTT

proud mother of GEORGE BRYANT

Vrouw in actie #23:
De beendruk met
knieklem na knokkelstoot
op handrug.

Margje de Koning /
Regisseur /
Tel: (31) 20 6798103 /
Fax: (31) 20 6767574 /
Mobile: (31) 6 24608776 /
Hemonylaan 12 /
1074 BG Amsterdam /

Vrouw in actie #16:
De polsblokkage met
achterwaartse armdraai.

Vrouw in actie #38:
De schoudertorsie met
beenworp.

Design
KesselsKramer

For
Margje de Koning_
Director_
Amsterdam,
The Netherlands

Info
Stock photos of women's self-defence moves are appropriated
for this film director's card. Working in a man's world she learnt
to "act tough", while her femininity is stressed via a pastel backdrop.

310k
paul rickus
me@310k.nl
+31(0)614663774

www.310k.nl

310k
ivo schmetz
we@310k.nl
+31 (0)6 22616985

www.310k.nl

Design/photography
310k
Paul Rickus_
Ivo Schmetz

For
310k_
Designers_
Amsterdam,
The Netherlands

Info
This duo dress up for the camera to celebrate the kitscher aspects of Alpine culture.

brighten the corners

brighten the corners

brighten the corners

brighten the corners

brighten the corners

brighten the corners

brighten the corners

brighten the corners

brighten the corners | studio for design
united kingdom unit 243 the bon marché centre
241-251 ferndale road london sw9 8bj
tel +44 (0)20 7274 4949 fax +44 (0)20 7738 5555
germany lindenspürstraße 32 70176 stuttgart
tel +49 (0)711 3 05 68 31 fax +49 (0)711 2 28 71 49

frank@brightenthecorners.com
m +49 (0)160 5536 117

frank philippin MA RCA

brighten the corners

brighten the corners

brighten the corners

brighten the corners

brighten the corners

brighten the corners

brighten the corners

Design/photography
Brighten the Corners
Frank Philippin_
Billy Kiossoglou

For
Brighten the Corners_
Designers_
London, UK_
Stuttgart, Germany

Info
For maximum flexibility this entire stationery system is printed
as stickers, to be used as letterheads or cards. The address sticker
changes colour as details alter, while imagery is tailored to
the individual on the receiving end. This system also acts as
a snapshot showcase for Brighten the Corners' photography.

x-act

x-act

x-act ag eventmarketing grubenstrasse 11 p.o. box ch-8045 zürich
welcome@x-act-event.ch www.x-act-event.ch
phone +41 1 4666070 fax +41 1 4666077

Design/photography   For   Info
Code.ch   X-act_   Carefully staged, atmospheric shots of rooms and situations
Reto Gehrig_   Event marketing_   emphasize this events agency's expertise.
Myriam Köstli   Zurich, Switzerland

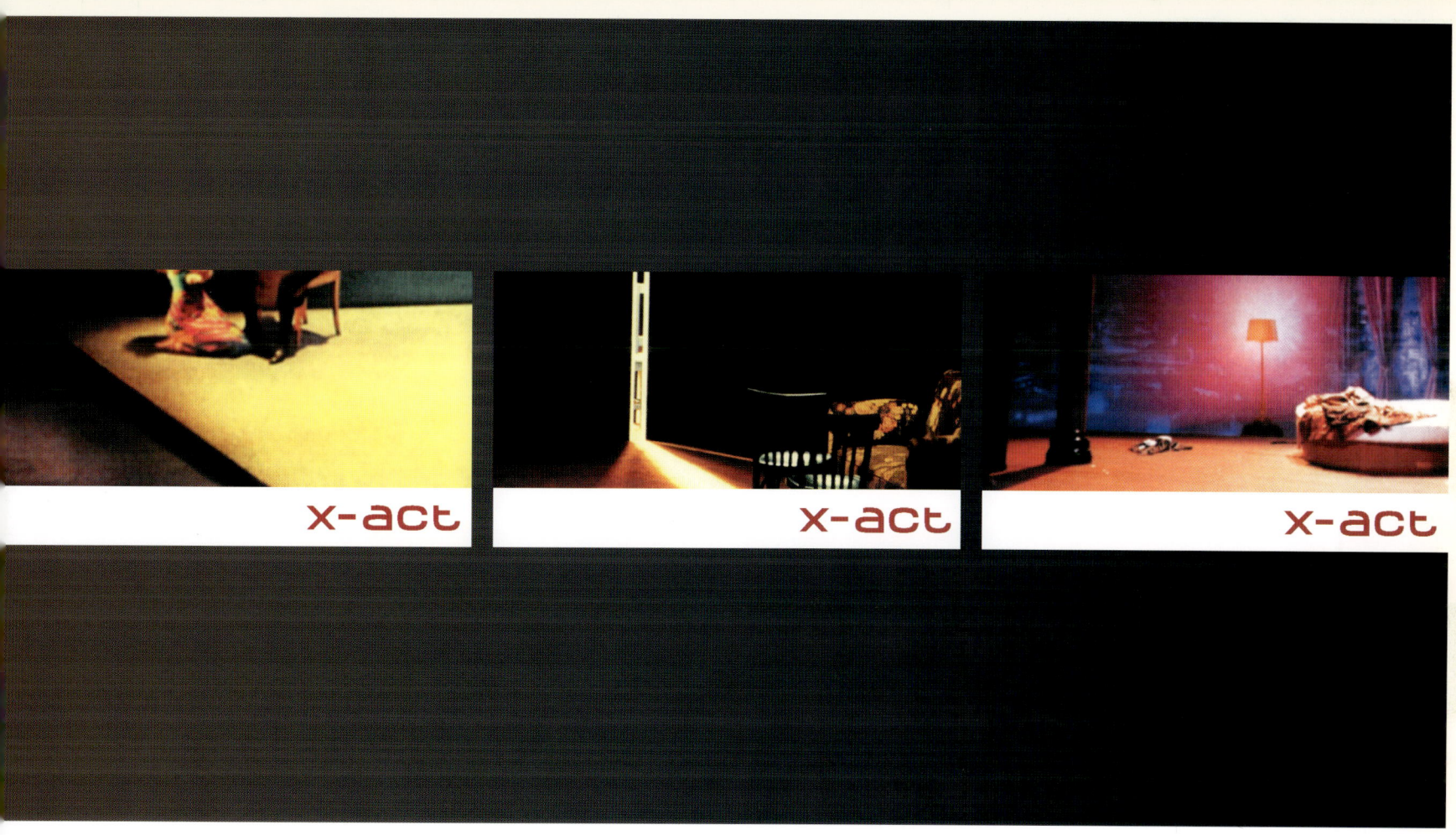

lauriergracht 39 / p.o.box 10007 /
1001 ea amsterdam / the netherlands

(poster campaign / Smartlappen festival)

kesselskramer

phone +31(0)20 5301060 /
fax +31(0)20 5301061 / church@kesselskramer.com

(tv commercial / ONVZ)

lauriergracht 39 / p.o.box 10007 /
1001 ea amsterdam / the netherlands

(print & poster campaign / Diesel)

kesselskramer

phone +31(0)20 5301060 /
fax +31(0)20 5301061 / church@kesselskramer.com

(print campaign / Ben)

Design
KesselsKramer

For
KesselsKramer_
Communications
agency_
Amsterdam,
The Netherlands

Info
Declaring themselves "only as good as their last work", images
borrowed from past projects create a constantly evolving
portfolio of double-sided cards.

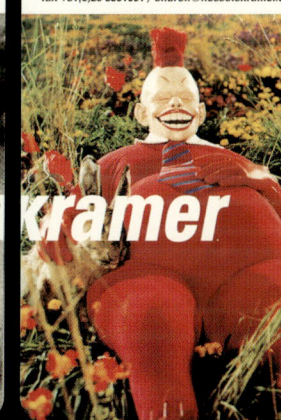

lauriergracht 39 / p.o.box 10007 /
1001 ea amsterdam / the netherlands

(tv commercial / Ben)

kesselskramer

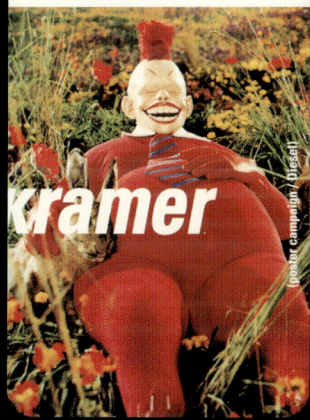

phone +31(0)20 5301060 /
fax +31(0)20 5301061 / church@kesselskramer.com

(poster campaign / Diesel)

lauriergracht 39 / p.o.box 10007 /
1001 ea amsterdam / the netherlands

(print & poster campaign / Diesel)

kesselskramer

phone +31(0)20 5301060 /
fax +31(0)20 5301061 / church@kesselskramer.com

(print campaign / Ben)

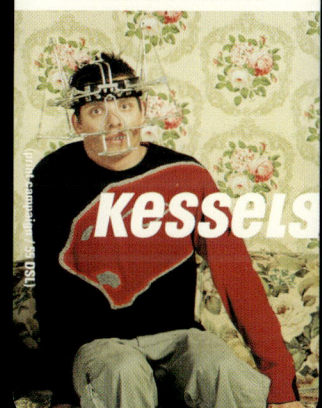

lauriergracht 39 / p.o.box 10007 /
1001 ea amsterdam / the netherlands

(tv commercial / DSL)

kesselskramer

phone +31(0)20 5301060 /
fax +31(0)20 5301061 / church@kesselskramer.com

(poster campaign / Ben)

lauriergracht 39 / p.o.box 10007 /
1001 ea amsterdam / the netherlands

(poster campaign / Ben)

kesselskramer

phone +31(0)20 5301060 /
fax +31(0)20 5301061 / church@kesselskramer.com

(poster campaign / Smaflapjen festival)

lauriergracht 39 / p.o.box 10007 /
1001 ea amsterdam / the netherlands

(do i.t. / booklet & exhibition)

phone +31(0)20 5301060 /
fax +31(0)20 5301061 / church@kesselskramer.com

kessels kramer

lauriergracht 39 / p.o.box 10007 /
1001 ea amsterdam / the netherlands

(print & poster campaign / Pazzua Arnhem)

kessels kramer

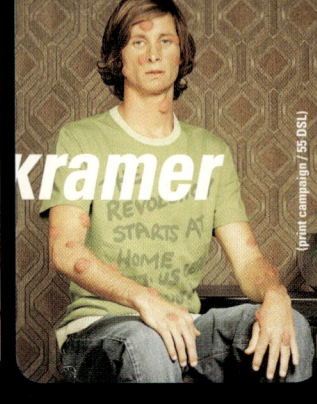

phone +31(0)20 5301060 /
fax +31(0)20 5301061 / church@kesselskramer.com

(print campaign / 55 DSL)

lauriergracht 39 / p.o.box 10007 /
1001 ea amsterdam / the netherlands

(poster campaign / Diesel)

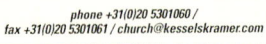

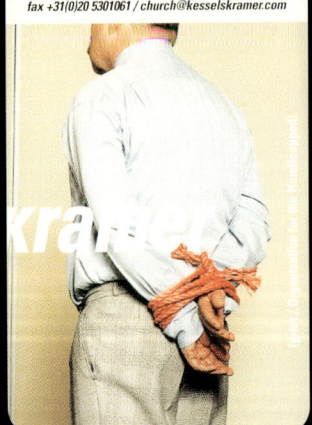

phone +31(0)20 5301060 /
fax +31(0)20 5301061 / church@kesselskramer.com

(print / Hans anten for the Handicapped)

kessels kramer

lauriergracht 39 / p.o.box 10007 /
1001 ea amsterdam / the netherlands

(tv commercial / Ben)

kessels kramer

phone +31(0)20 5301060 /
fax +31(0)20 5301061 / church@kesselskramer.com

(poster campaign / Ben)

lauriergracht 39 / p.o.box 10007 /
1001 ea amsterdam / the netherlands

phone +31(0)20 5301060 /
fax +31(0)20 5301061 / church@kesselskramer.com

lauriergracht 39 / p.o.box 10007 /
1001 ea amsterdam / the netherlands

phone +31(0)20 5301060 /
fax +31(0)20 5301061 / church@kesselskramer.com

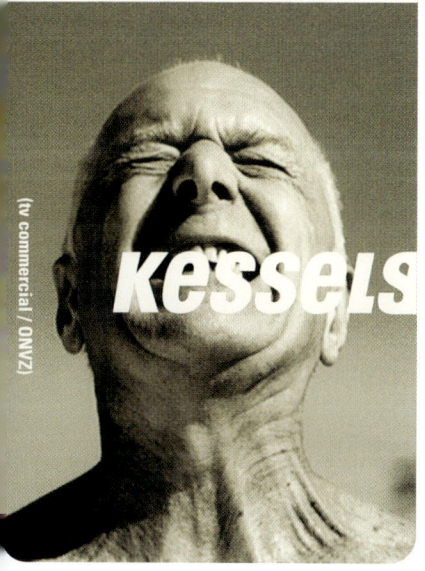

(tv commercial / ONVZ)

(poster campaign / Ben)

(poster for the Handicapped)

(print & poster campaign / Diesel)

kessels**kramer**

kessels**kramer**

love: skiing
hate: being shouted at

love: family fortunes
hate: marzipan

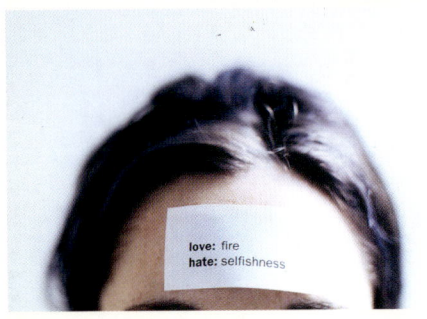

love: fire
hate: selfishness

love: lipstick
hate: mushrooms

love: lily
hate: arsenal

love: fraser
hate: my neighbours

Design/photography
Studio Myerscough

For
Studio Myerscough_
Designers_
London, UK

Info
Each member of the studio wrote their pet hate and passionate love on a piece of paper and stuck it to their forehead; the resulting "anonymous" portraits offer an insight into their personalities without being overly familiar. This version of a traditional parlour game is a sure-fire ice-breaker at meetings!

Design/photography
Kerr Noble

For
General Public_
Creative
consultancy_
London, UK

Info
An identity of images collected from the general public and
used copyright-free emphasizes this agency's aim to enrich
the environment. Via the business cards Kerr Noble explore
common space through abstract colour compositions.

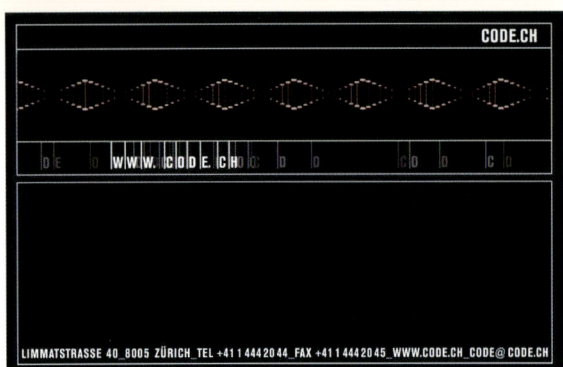

CODE.CH

WWW.CODE.CH

LIMMATSTRASSE 40_8005 ZÜRICH_TEL +41 1 444 20 44_FAX +41 1 444 20 45_WWW.CODE.CH_CODE@ CODE.CH

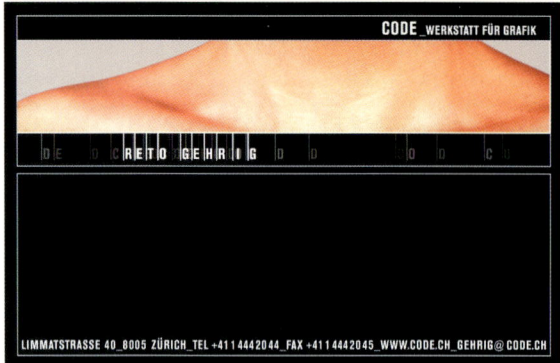

CODE_WERKSTATT FÜR GRAFIK

RETO GEHRIG

LIMMATSTRASSE 40_8005 ZÜRICH_TEL +41 1 444 20 44_FAX +41 1 444 20 45_WWW.CODE.CH_GEHRIG@ CODE.CH

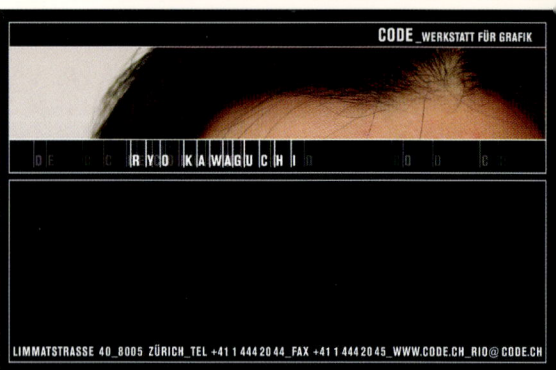

CODE_WERKSTATT FÜR GRAFIK

RYO KAWAGUCHI

LIMMATSTRASSE 40_8005 ZÜRICH_TEL +41 1 444 20 44_FAX +41 1 444 20 45_WWW.CODE.CH_RIO@ CODE.CH

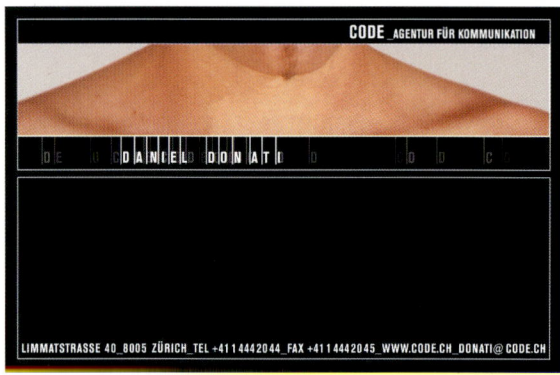

CODE_AGENTUR FÜR KOMMUNIKATION

DANIEL DONATI

LIMMATSTRASSE 40_8005 ZÜRICH_TEL +41 1 444 20 44_FAX +41 1 444 20 45_WWW.CODE.CH_DONATI@ CODE.CH

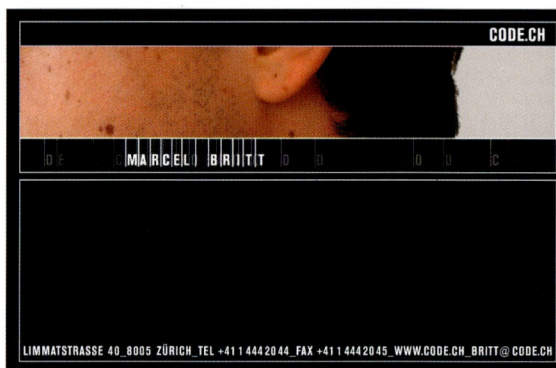

CODE.CH

MARCEL BRITT

LIMMATSTRASSE 40_8005 ZÜRICH_TEL +41 1 444 20 44_FAX +41 1 444 20 45_WWW.CODE.CH_BRITT@ CODE.CH

Design/photography
Code.ch

For
Code.ch_
Designers_
Zurich,
Switzerland

Info
Each member of Code.ch chose an identifying but anonymous
part of their body to be photographed and featured. Cropped
into a "bar-code" format, it hints that a secret language, or code,
is in use.

CODE _AGENTUR FÜR KOMMUNIKATION

DE M Y R I A M K Ö S T L I O D O D C

LIMMATSTR. 40_8005 ZÜRICH_TEL +41 1 444 20 44_FAX +41 1 444 20 45_WWW.CODE.CH_MYRIAM@CODE.CH

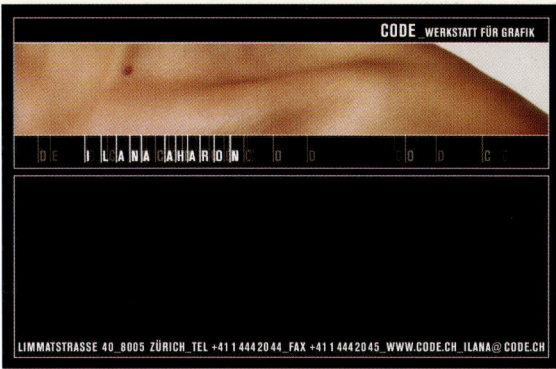

CODE _WERKSTATT FÜR GRAFIK

DE I L A N A A H A R O N C D O D C

LIMMATSTRASSE 40_8005 ZÜRICH_TEL +41 1 444 20 44_FAX +41 1 444 20 45_WWW.CODE.CH_ILANA@CODE.CH

CODE _AGENTUR FÜR KOMMUNIKATION

DE R O B E R T H A R T M A N N D O D C

LIMMATSTRASSE 40_8005 ZÜRICH_TEL +41 1 444 20 44_FAX +41 1 444 20 45_WWW.CODE.CH_ROB@CODE.CH

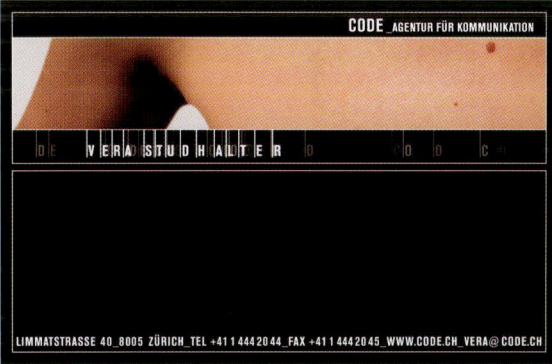

CODE _AGENTUR FÜR KOMMUNIKATION

DE V E R A S T U D H A L T E R D O D C

LIMMATSTRASSE 40_8005 ZÜRICH_TEL +41 1 444 20 44_FAX +41 1 444 20 45_WWW.CODE.CH_VERA@CODE.CH

Design
  KesselsKramer
Photography
  Bianca Pilet

For
  do_
  Advertising
  agency_
  Amsterdam,
  The Netherlands

Info
A fictitious brand, "do" may be applied to any product, event
or undertaking its protagonists imagine. This ambiguity is
hinted at via the use of show-through on a semi-transparent
stock.

lauriergracht 39
1016 rg amsterdam
p.o. box 3240
1001 aa amsterdam
the netherlands
phone +31(0)20 5301070
fax +31(0)20 5301061
e-mail domail@dosurf.com
website www.dosurf.com

197

fabric | ch

electronic architecture

info@fabric.ch   http://www.fabric.ch
langallerie 6 | 1003 lausanne | switzerland
t. +41 (0) 21 351 1020 | f. +41 (0) 21 351 1022

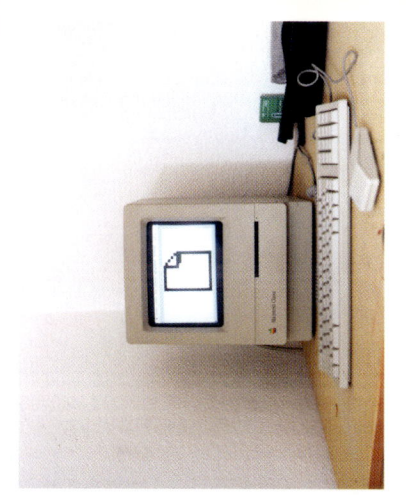

<u>Design/photography</u>
Happypets Products

<u>For</u>
Fabric.ch_
Electronic architects_
Lausanne,
Switzerland

<u>Info</u>
For these "electronic architects", Happypets bring the computer's "document" icon into the real world. By placing it in various familiar and surreal situations, the aim is to demonstrate their client's versatility and relevance.

Christian Küsters CHK Design

Design
 CHK Design
 Christian Küsters
Photography
 Sølve Sunsbø

For
 CHK Design_
 Designer_
 London, UK

Info
"I simply ran out of business cards, which is surprising considering
how many you have to get printed each time. I usually get bored
of the old one before then." Christian needed some cards in a
hurry, and used the image from his recent book cover. Surprising
too that it works as a cover and a card. This complex digital
deconstruction is just as arresting shrunk to card size.

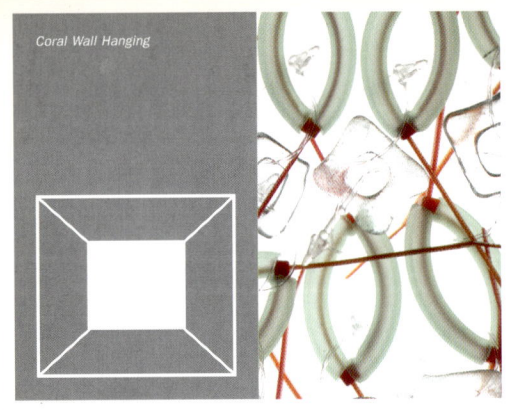

Coral Wall Hanging

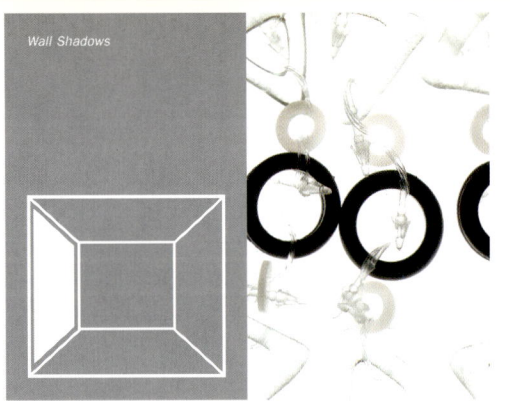

Wall Shadows

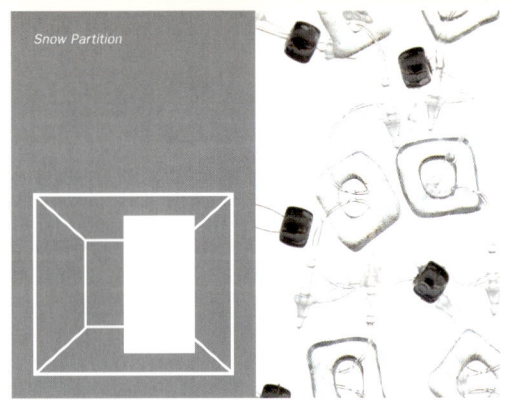

Snow Partition

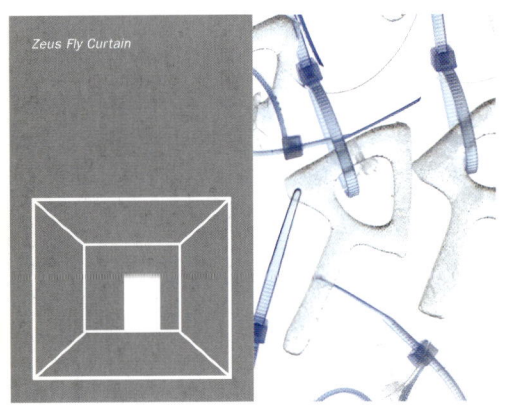

Zeus Fly Curtain

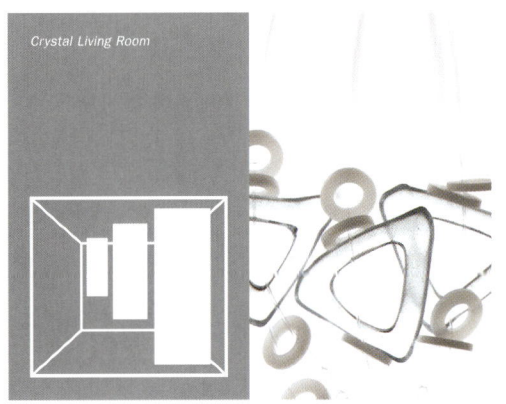

Crystal Living Room

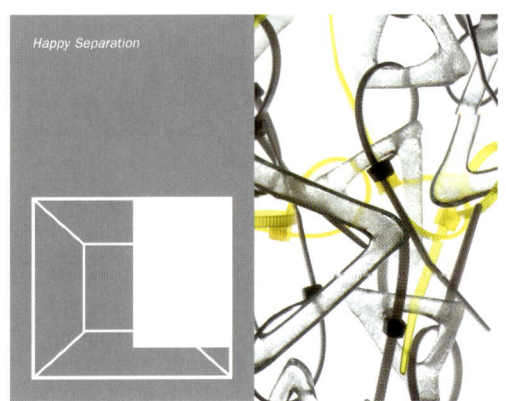

Happy Separation

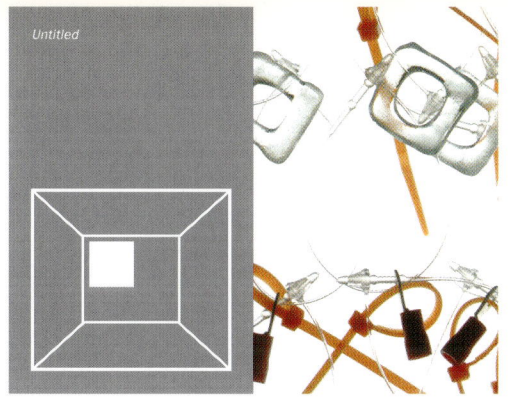

Untitled

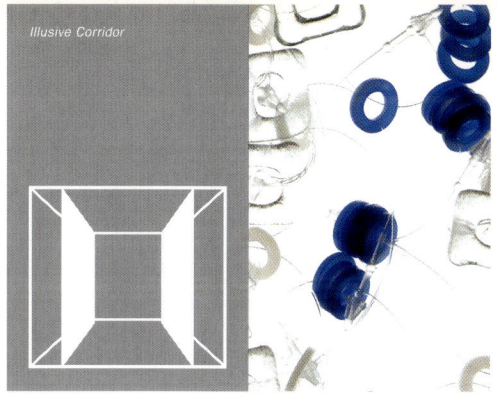

Illusive Corridor

Virtual Pearl

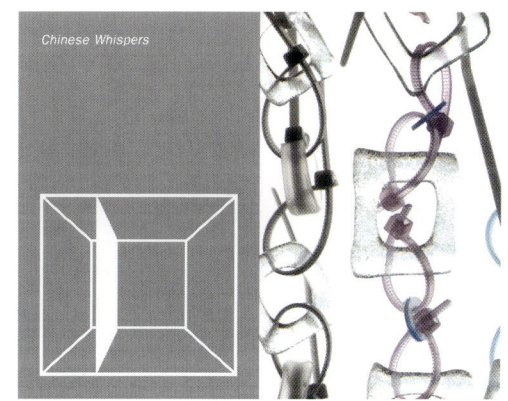

Chinese Whispers

Ruth Spaak
Glass Interventions

Walnut Tree House
20 Sandfield Road
Stratford-upon-Avon
Warwickshire CV37 9AG
Phone 01789 415244
www.axisartists.org.uk

<u>Design</u>
Brighten the Corners
Frank Philippin_
Billy Kiossoglou

<u>For</u>
Ruth Spaak_
Glass designer_
Stratford-upon-Avon,
UK

<u>Info</u>
The diagrams suggest how glass designer Ruth Spaak's "curtains" may be positioned within a room, while photography shows the multi-various elements at actual size.

Design
 CDT Design
 Iain Crockart
 Stuart Youngs
Photography
 Nick Veasey

For
 186k_
 IT Networks_
 Reading, UK

Info
 Operating a state-of-the-art fibre-optic network, 186k spread information at the speed of light. Designers CDT provide them with an ever-changing library of light-based images, and each staff member receives a set of cards featuring various effects.

Martin Benké
Network Operations Director
Email martin.benke186k.co.uk
Direct 0118 906 4168
Mobile 07768 865266

186k Limited
The Spectrum Queens Road Reading Berkshire RG1 4BQ
Tel 0118 906 4000 Fax 0118 906 4411 www.186k.co.uk

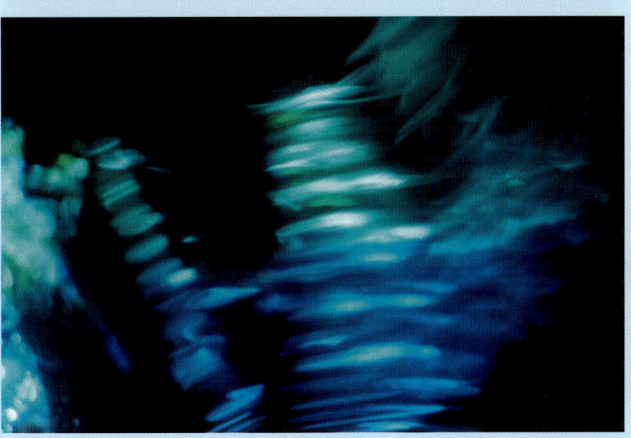

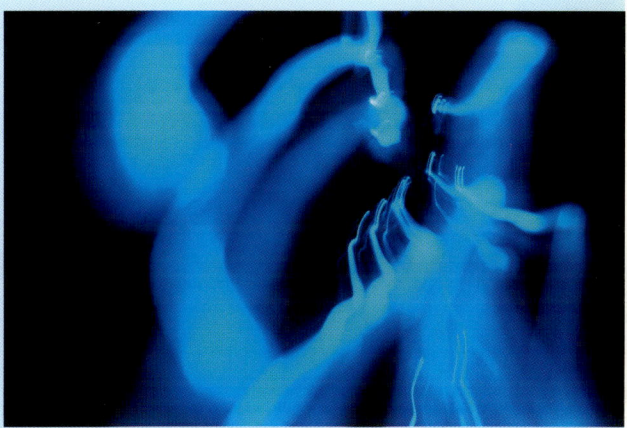

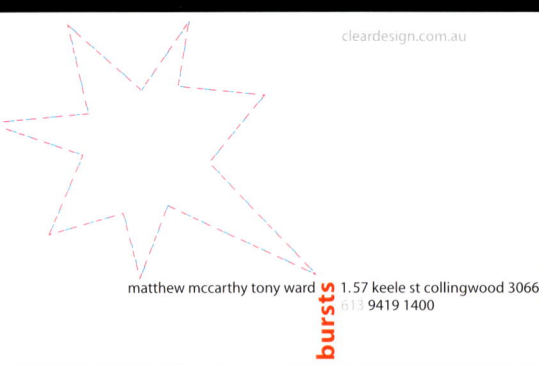

cleardesign.com.au

matthew mccarthy tony ward 1.57 keele st collingwood 3066
bursts 613 9419 1400

Design
Bursts
Matthew McCarthy_
Tony Ward

For
Bursts_
Magazine_
Melbourne,
Australia

Info
Printed alongside the actual zine *Bursts*, images are taken from
the publication and the same single-sided coated stock was
used, printed four-colour over one-colour.

Jake Tilson

16 Talfourd Road London SE15 5NY

T 7701 7245
F 7703 9860

www.thecooker.com
www.areaatlas.com

jake@thecooker.com

T 7701 7245
F 7703 9860

16 Talfourd Road London SE15 5NY

jake@thecooker.com

www.thecooker.com
www.areaatlas.com

Jake Tilson

Design/photography
Jake Tilson

For
Jake Tilson_
Designer_
London, UK

Info
A love of food and travel inspires Jake's many and varied
business cards.

fréd&rique Daubal
haarlemmerdijk 31-1 hoog
1013 ka amsterdam - nl
phone +31(0)20 427 4907
e-mail fredd@xs4all.nl

3 22 SEPT 96

<u>Design</u>
  Frédérique Daubal

<u>For</u>
  Frédérique Daubal_
  Designer_
  Amsterdam,
  The Netherlands

<u>Info</u>
  An ad-hoc solution for a temporary address; Frédérique
  rubber-stamps fragments of snapshots from her travels.

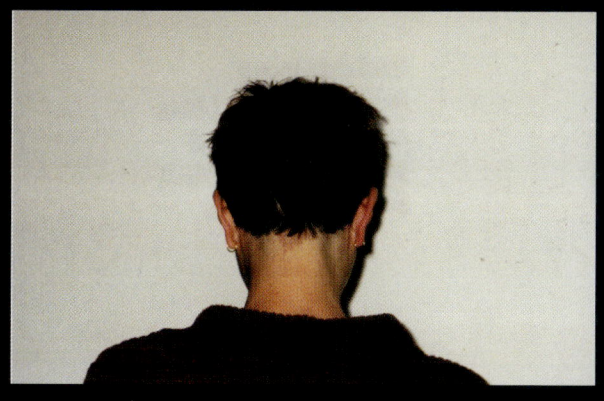

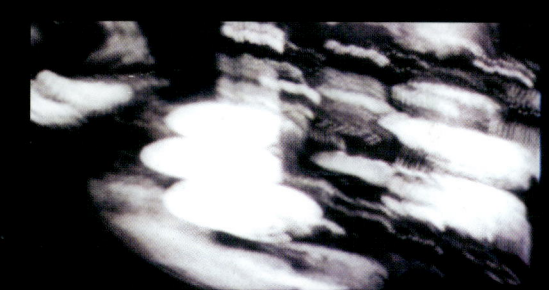

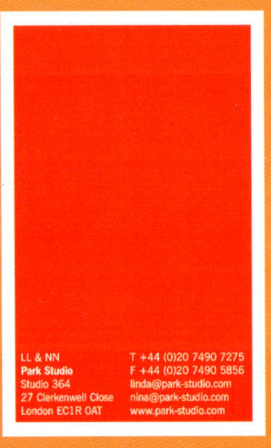

Design/photography
Park Studio
Linda Lundin_
Nina Nägel

For
Park Studio_
Designers_
London, UK

Info
Believing that handing out business cards is "too formal and lacking in genuine interaction", Linda and Nina left a convenient blank space on theirs, in which to add a personal message or spontaneous drawing.

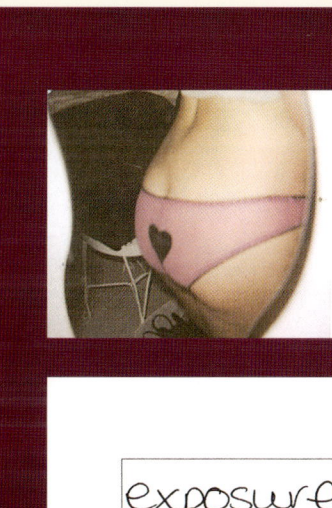

HANNAH GRANT EXPOSURE 22-23 LITTLE PORTLAND STREET LONDON W1W 8BU
T 020 7907 7130 DIRECT T 020 7907 7146 F 020 7907 7131
M 07740 513670 E HANNAH@EXPOSURELTD.COM

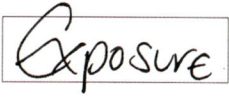

TRACIE-JAYNE SULLIVAN
EXPOSURE 22-23 LITTLE PORTLAND STREET LONDON W1W 8BU
T 020 7907 7130 DIRECT T 020 7907 7132 F 020 7907 7131
E TRACIE@EXPOSURELTD.COM

MELANIE RUSHWORTH EXPOSURE 22-23 LITTLE PORTLAND STREET LONDON W1W 8BU
T 020 7907 7130 DIRECT T 020 7907 7135 F 020 7907 7131
E MELANIE@EXPOSURELTD.COM

SARAH BRUCE
EXPOSURE 22-23 LITTLE PORTLAND STREET LONDON W1W 8BU
T 020 7907 7130 DIRECT T 020 7907 7279 F 020 7907 7131
M 07967 681 889 E SARAHB@EXPOSURELTD.COM

Design
Exposure

For
Exposure_
Communications
agency_
London, UK

Info
Each individual chooses an image and renders the company
name in their own handwriting.

211

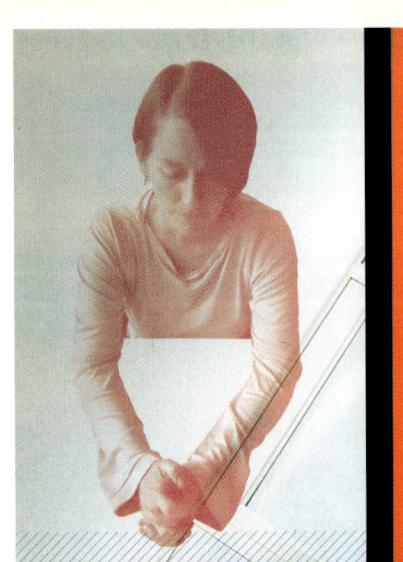
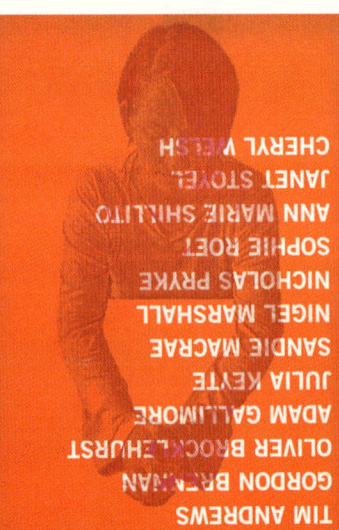

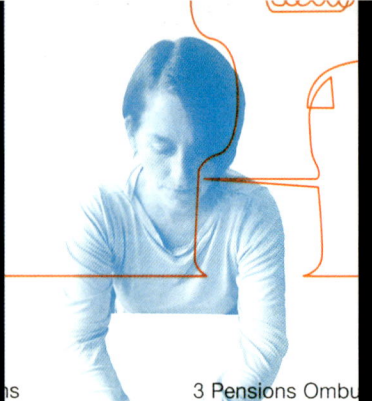
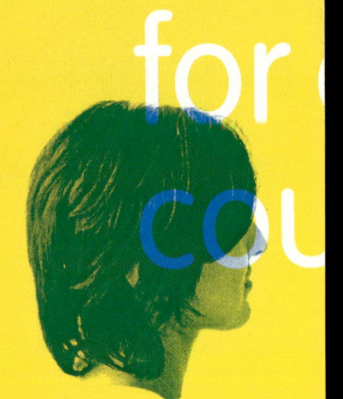

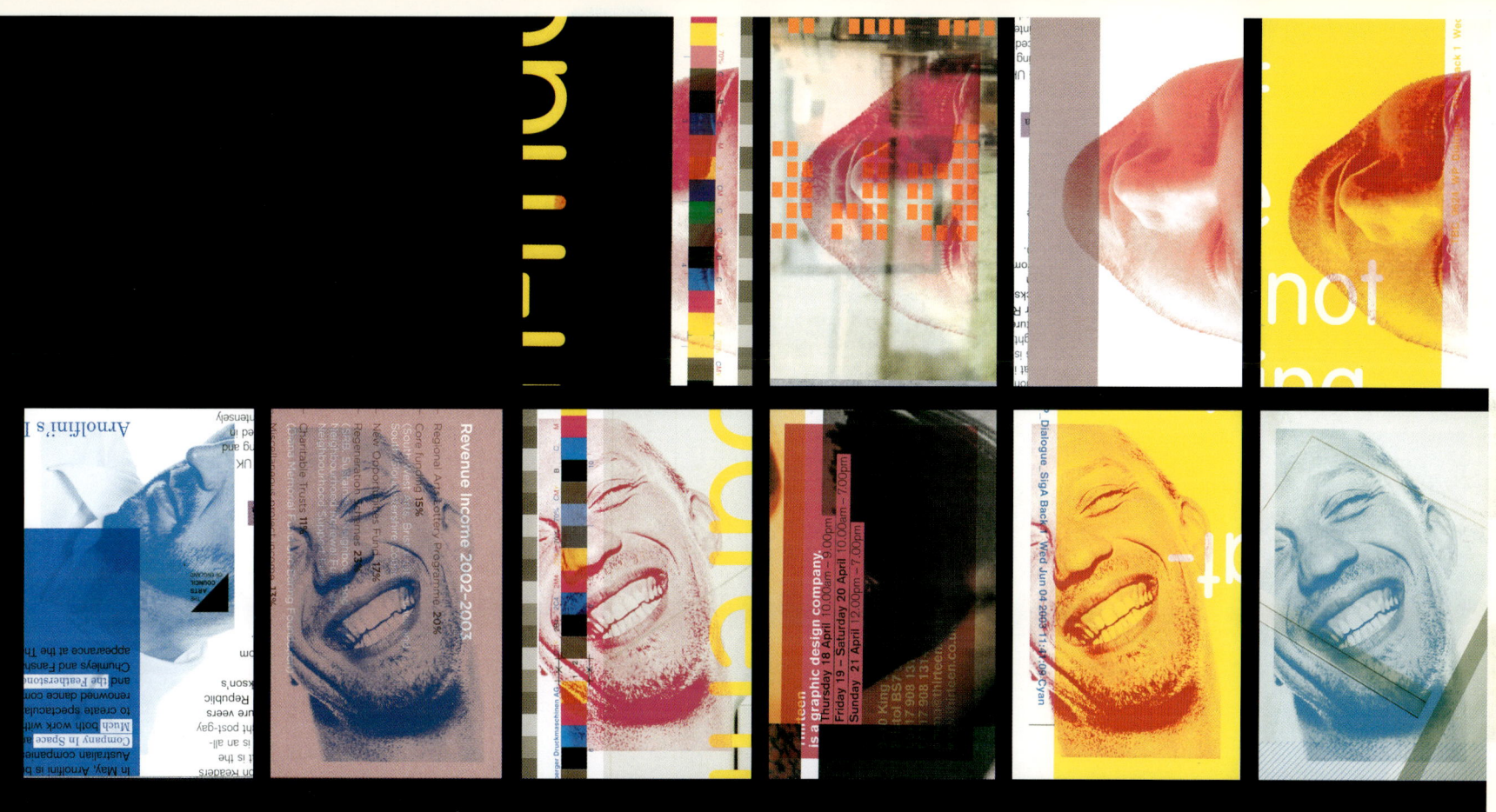

Design/photography
Thirteen

For
Thirteen_
Designers_
Bristol, UK

Info
Appropriating running sheets from past jobs, Thirteen initiated an "accidental business card project". Using a large-format Hewlett-Packard inkjet printer (which they're test driving), evocative portraits and personal details are added in one or many colours; no two cards are the same, yet the finish is far from DIY.

V1r+u@| Hum@|\(01)$

Saturday 18 May 8.00pm
Company in Space
CO3

Friday 24 May 8.00pm
Willi Dorner
Mazy

Saturday 8 June 8.00pm
Company Q
CHARNIK-1

Wednesday 12 June 8.00pm – 1.00am
Location: Thekla, the Grove, Bristol
The Cholmondeleys and The
Featherstonehaughs
One and a Half: The Club Shows

Friday 14 June 4:00pm
Edward Scheer
lecture

Anja Lutz ★ Grafische Gestaltung ★ Chorinerstrasse ██ 10435 Berlin
Telefon (030) 275 96 100 ★ Fax (030) 275 96 101 ★ anja@shift.de

Design
  Anja Lutz

For
  Anja Lutz_
  Designer_
  Berlin, Germany

Info
  Based in a one-time "East" district of Berlin, Anja revels in the
  time-warp imagery still found in her fast-changing neighbourhood.
  Sun-bleached photos, kitsch stock and pre-digital typefaces are
  combined into a celebration.

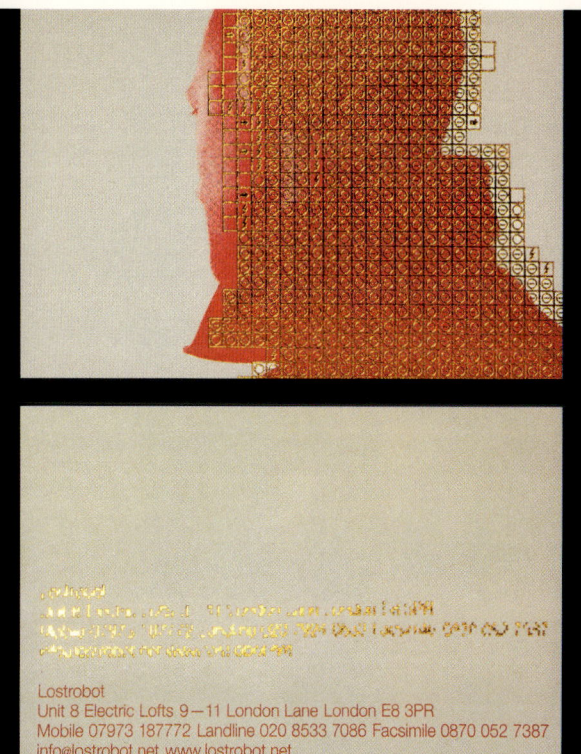

Lostrobot
Unit 8 Electric Lofts 9—11 London Lane London E8 3PR
Mobile 07973 187772 Landline 020 8533 7086 Facsimile 0870 052 7387
info@lostrobot.net www.lostrobot.net

Design
Mode

For
Lostrobot_
Photographers_
London, UK

Info
Slightly green-tinted stock, red duotone and a bronze foil emboss
create intimate portraiture in a calm space overlaid with techno-
patination (of light meter symbols). Individual cards offer phone
and email, while an address card includes a pixellated, metallic
and unreadable (by humans?) set of details.

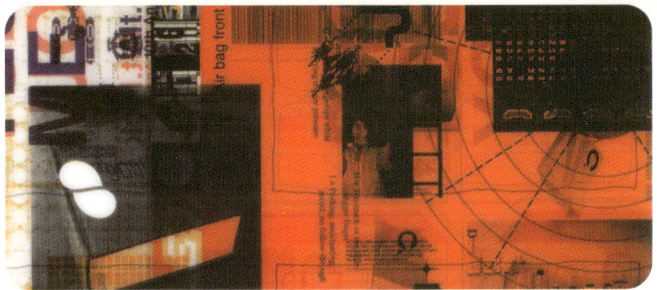

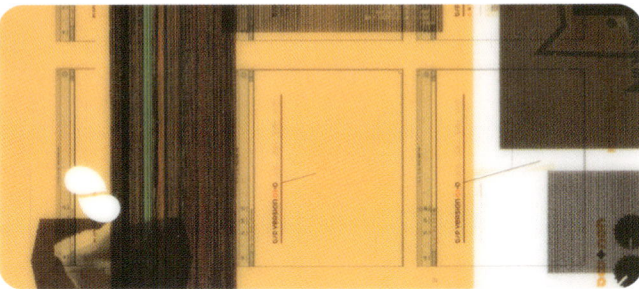
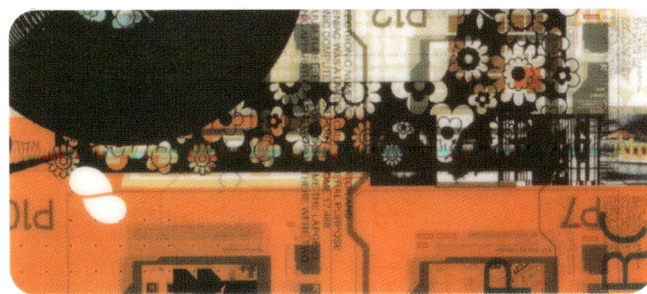

<u>Design</u>
Segura Inc

<u>For</u>
Segura Inc_
Designers_
Chicago, USA

<u>Info</u>
A unique, satin-finished plastic in a slim format is used for this series of cards. Densely-layered imagery appears embedded within this surface, while on the reverse, subtle grey type floats on a creamy ground. The effect is of extreme precision married to intense creativity.

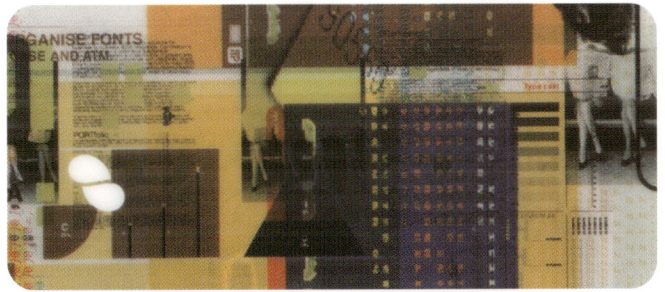

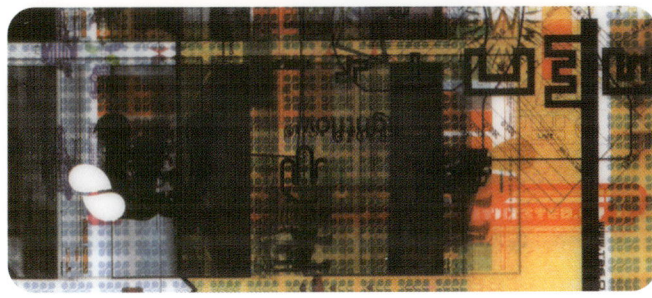

carlos segura
carlos@segura-inc.com

www.segura-inc.com

1110 north milwaukee avenue
chicago, illinois 60622.4017 usa
773.862.5667 w 773.862.1214 f
773.960.9673 c

Richard and Chris.

Design
  Yacht Associates
  Richard Bull_
  Christopher Thompson

For
  Yacht Associates_
  Designers_
  London, UK

Info
  Presented inside a mini folder, like an upmarket restaurant bill,
  Yacht's cool, white "credit card" includes an embossed phone
  number and signature strip, for each partner's handwritten
  addition.

Tim Watson

tim.watson@duffy.com

DUFFY / LONDON

POSITION MANAGING DIRECTOR

Design
Duffy
Joe Duffy_
Alan Leusink_
Neil Powell_
Tom Riddle

For
Duffy_
Designers_
Minneapolis/New
York, USA; London,
UK; Singapore;
Hong Kong

Info
One die is used to cut all the metal cards for Duffy's five offices worldwide, while each location has its own distinctly subtle colour palette, used for the add-on stickers. The notches align, stressing connectivity and collaboration between teams.

Form®

47 Tabernacle Street
London EC2A 4AA, UK

Telephone: +44 (0)20 7014 1430
Fax: +44 (0)20 7014 1431
ISDN: +44 (0)20 7014 1432

Email: paula@form.uk.com
Web: www.form.uk.com

Design
Form

For
Form_
Designers_
London, UK

Info
The simplest layout made memorable; Form's etched and
die-cut aluminium cards are constantly evolving but instantly
recognizable.

Paul Wesley Griggs
07771 784 622

Design
Lucky 37
Paul Wesley Griggs

For
Lucky 37_
Photographer_
London, UK

Info
Paul worked on this card with a company that makes circuit
boards, exploring and experimenting with a process that
includes photo acid etching, silk-screen printing, routing and
drilling; variations also occur in the mixing of ink colours and
the density of fibreglass.

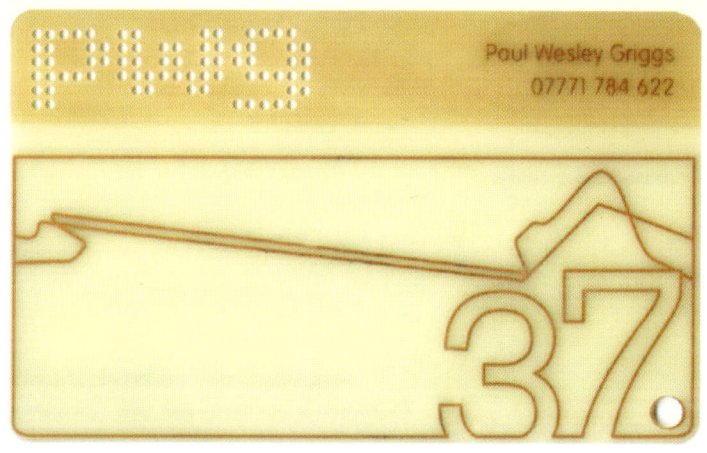

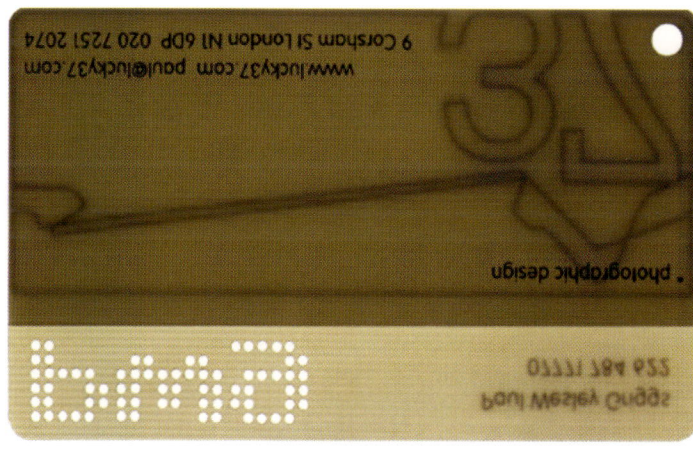

Paul Wesley Griggs
07771 784 622

37.

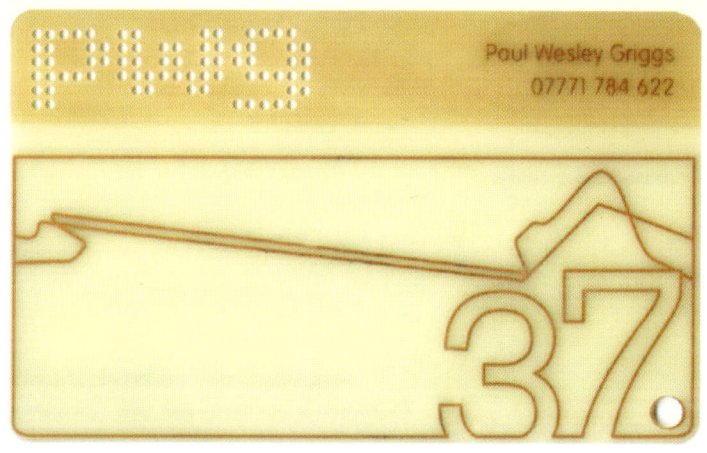

Paul Wesley Griggs
07771 784 622

37.

9 Corsham St London N1 6DP 020 7251 2074
www.lucky37.com paul@lucky37.com

photographic design

Paul Wesley Griggs
07771 784 622

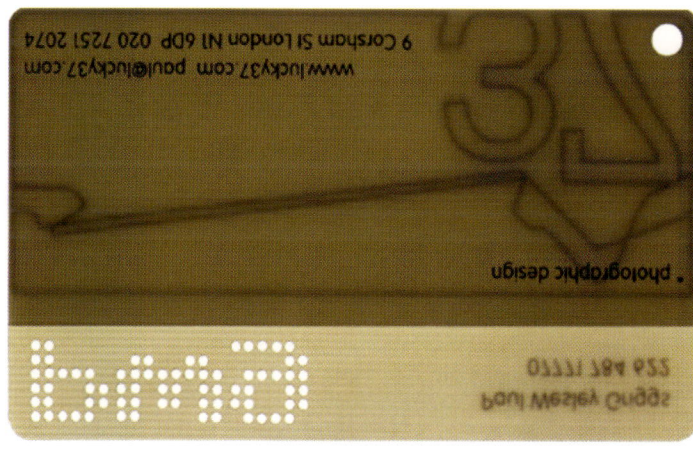

9 Corsham St London N1 6DP 020 7251 2074
www.lucky37.com paul@lucky37.com

photographic design

Paul Wesley Griggs
07771 784 622

Design
 Duffy
 Hugh Tarpey

For
 Unity_
 Media agency_
 London, UK

Info
 Wanting to appear both professional and fun, the no-nonsense
 Unity logo is combined with a printed plastic sleeve, creating
 an animated abstract as you extract the card.

Heads Inc.
So Takahashi
526 West 26th Street Suite 211 New York, NY 10001
Tel: 212 243 4102 Fax: 212 243 5544
email: soso@bway.net

Heads Inc.

So Takahashi

526 West 26th Street Suite 211 New York, NY 10001
Tel: 212 243 4102 Fax: 212 243 5544
email: soso@bway.net

Heads Inc.

So Takahashi

526 West 26th Street Suite 211 New York, NY 10001
Tel: 212 243 4102 Fax: 212 243 5544
email: soso@bway.net

Heads Inc.

So Takahashi

526 West 26th Street Suite 211 New York, NY 10001

Design
Heads Inc
So Takahashi

For
Heads Inc_
Designers_
New York, USA

Info
So's 5mm-thick plexiglass card makes a bold statement; plus
there's the added recognition factor of evoking an over-sized
Pantone chip. The end result is a welcome desk-top enhancement.

Big Active

Art Direction, Design
& Creative Management
Warehouse D4, Metropolitan Wharf,
Wapping Wall, London, E1W 3SS
Tel: (020) 7702 9365 Fax: (020) 7702 9366
www.bigactive.com

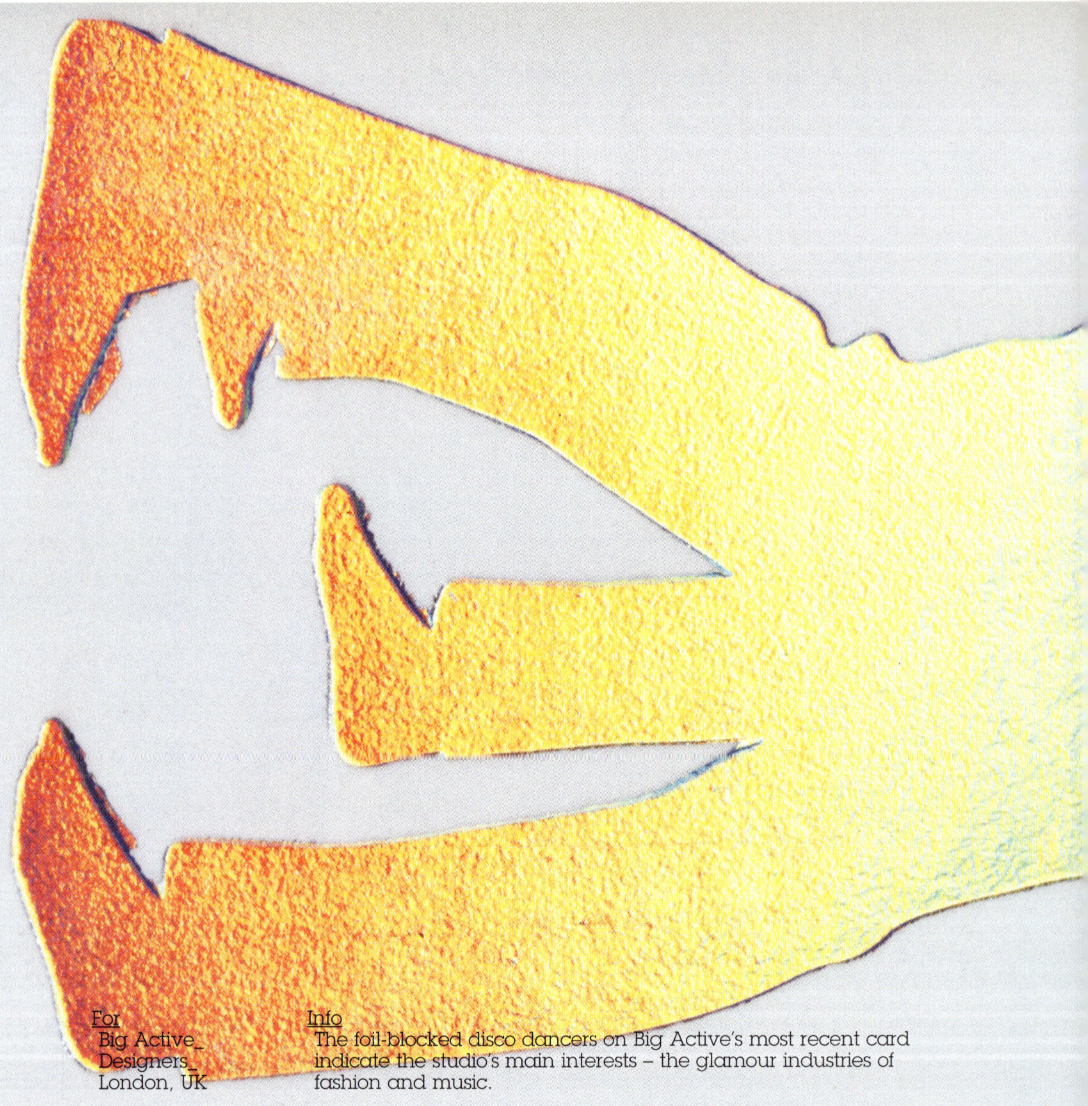

Design
Big Active

For
Big Active_
Designers_
London, UK

Info
The foil-blocked disco dancers on Big Active's most recent card
indicate the studio's main interests – the glamour industries of
fashion and music.

Martin Scofield
Chief Executive

Beyon
4th Floor
8 – 14 Vine Hill
London
EC1R 5DX

Telephone
+44 (0)20 7278 0207
Facsimile
+44 (0)20 7278 8043

martins@beyon.co.uk
www.beyon.co.uk

Design
SEA

For
Beyon_
Furniture
designers_
London, UK

Info
For a sophisticated furniture company, a simple marque
in a clutter-free zone recalls the purest forms of Modernism.

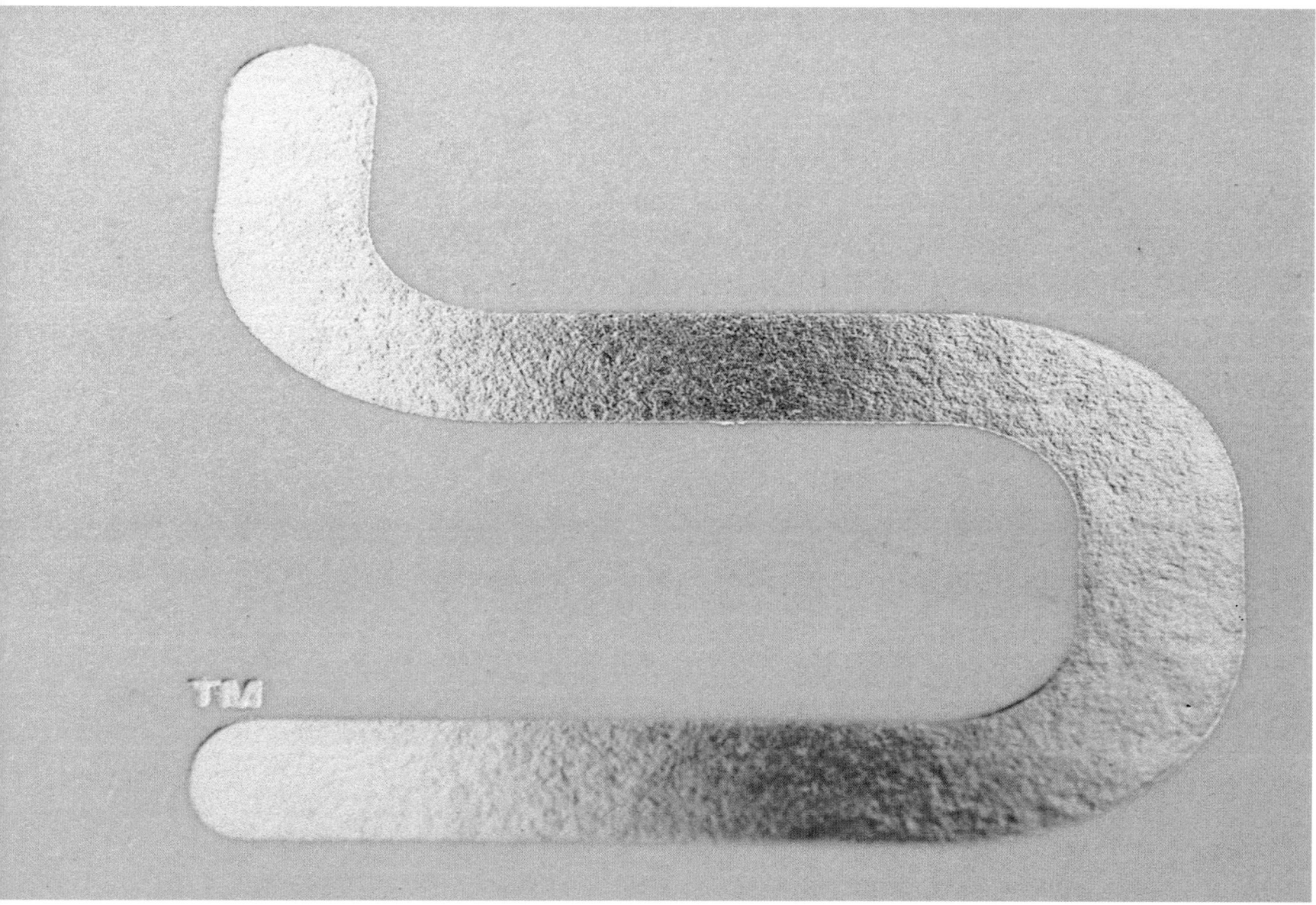

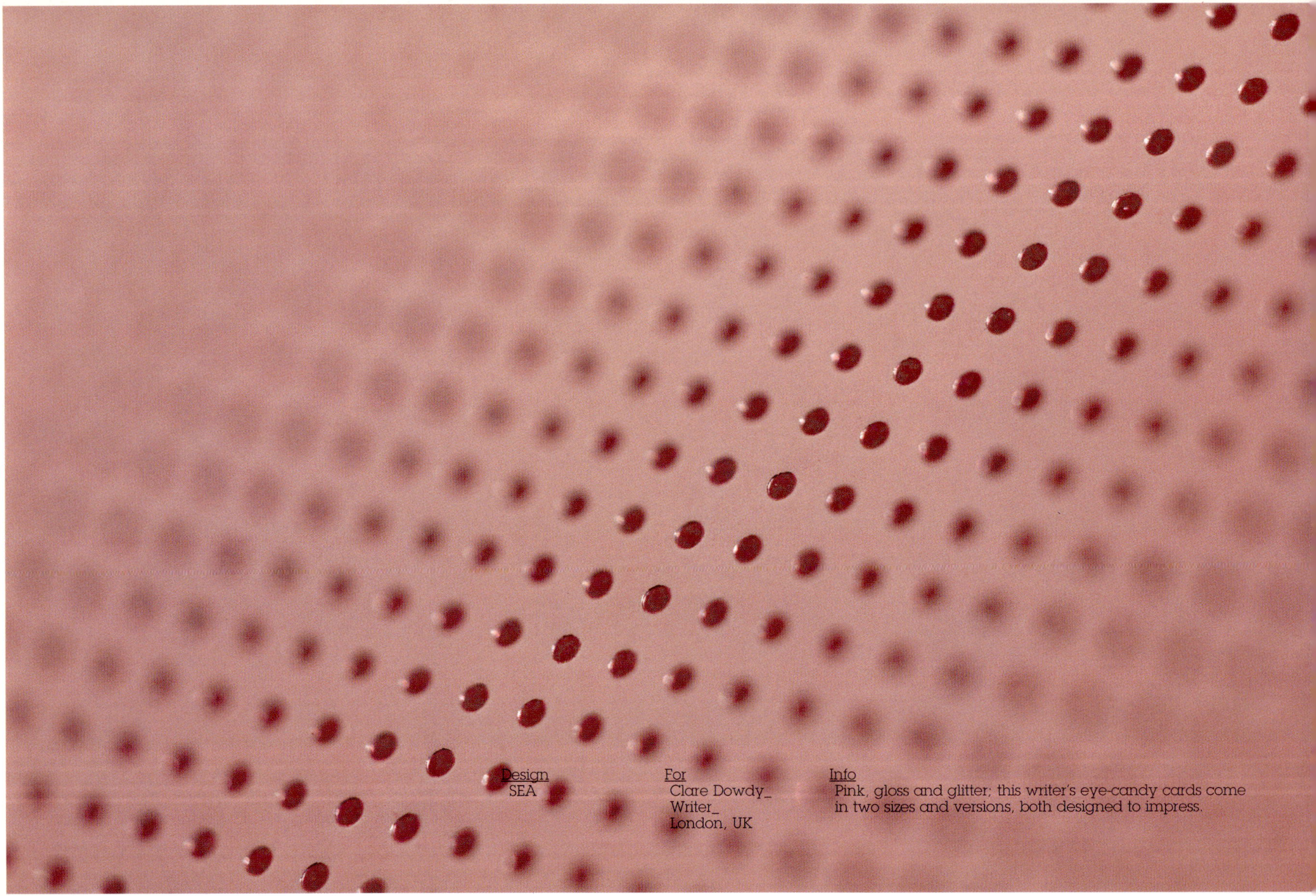

Design
SEA

For
Clare Dowdy_
Writer_
London, UK

Info
Pink, gloss and glitter; this writer's eye-candy cards come in two sizes and versions, both designed to impress.

Clare Dowdy
69 Great Russell Street
London WC1B 3BA
Telephone 020 7...
Mobile 07967...
claredowdy@...
...riter

Fold & glue

Intersection
Call DAN
+44(0)20 7549 8641

DAN

NEQ

Intersection
Call DAN
+44(0)20 7549 8641

NEQ

DAN

Intersection
Call DAN
+44(0)20 7549 8641

Intersection
Call DAN
+44(0)20 7549 8641

ROSS

Intersection

GUY BIRD
Deputy Editor
guy@intersectionmagazine.com

49-59 Old Street
London EC1V 9HX
tel +44 (0) 207 608 11 66
mob +44 (0) 797 964 6652
fax + 44 (0) 207 608 10 90
www.intersectionmagazine.com

<u>Design</u>
Yorgo Tloupas

<u>For</u>
Intersection_
Magazine_
London, UK

<u>Info</u>
A magazine that looks at the relevance of cars in daily life, *Intersection* redefined a publishing formula. Similarly, the designers questioned why a business card couldn't more closely reflect their concerns. With scalpel and glue, turn this die-cut plan into a favourite desk-top toy.

Jimmy Fok photographer ᵐ98586412

Calibre

213 Henderson Rd #02-01 Henderson Industrial Park Singapore 159553
ᵖ65. 6225 1005 ᶠ65. 6275 5845 ᵉjimmy@calibrepics.com ʷcalibrepics.com

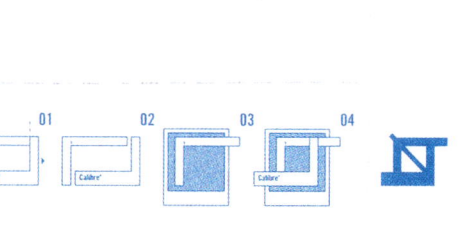

Design
  Kinetic
  Pann Lim_
  Roy Poh_
  Leng Soh

For
  Calibre_
  Photographer_
  Singapore

Info
  This photographer's card is minimal; but an unusual
  perforation transforms it into a "cropper".

Calibre

213 Henderson Rd #02-01 Henderson Industrial Park Singapore 159553
p 65. 6225 1005 f 65. 6275 5845 e jimmy@calibrepics.com w calibrepics.com

Jimmy Fok photographer m 98586412

blast

5 hanover yard   noel road   london   n1 8ya
tel 020 7359 7422   mobile 07768 743 202
martin@blast.co.uk / www.blast.co.uk

martin cox
director

Design
  Blast
  Matt Baxter_
  Martin Cox_
  Colin Gifford

For
  Blast_
  Designers_
  London, UK

Info
  The rocket's exhaust was created by burning each card
  by hand, while the logotype accentuates the idea of speed
  and space.

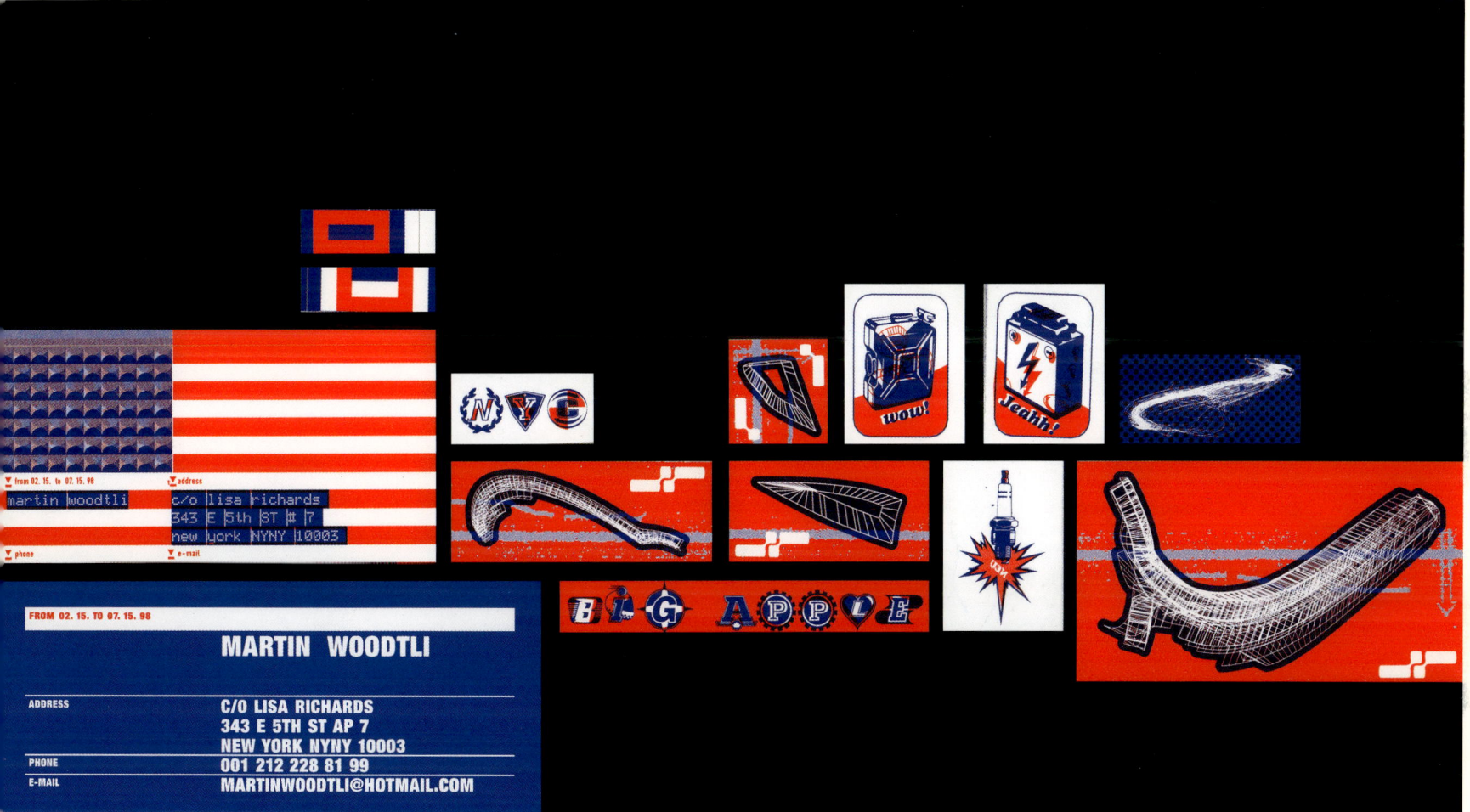

Design
  Martin Woodtli

For
  Martin Woodtli_
  Designer_
  New York, USA

Info
  A stamp-collecting bag full of small stickers and cards made
  highly visible by using fluorescent ink, announced Martin's
  temporary move to New York. The imagery is suitably dynamic.

Scrawl Collective
Illustration Agency
Exhibitions
Live Painting + Murals
Art Consultant

Contact :- Ric Blackshaw
+44 (0) 7770 888104
ric@scrawlcollective.co.uk

www.scrawlcollective.co.uk

Design
  Ric Blackshaw

For
  Scrawl Collective_
  Art Agency_
  London, UK

Info
  Ric's distinctive handwriting, and a doodled layout, point
  to the handmade aesthetic which underpins this unique,
  street-art-inspired illustration agency.

Design
Stefan Plaetz

For
Stefan Plaetz_
Artist/illustrator_
London, UK

Info
Known for his mural-sized compositions and for painting "live"
at special events, Stefan's card showcases his dynamic style.

Design/photography | For | Info
Celecao | Celecao_ | Graphic designer Boris Brumnjak wanted to emphasize the
Boris Brumnjak | T-shirt designer_ | DIY roots of his t-shirt company Celecao; he combined index
 | Berlin, Germany | cards, hand-written text and stationery stickers to create each
 | | unique example.

Design
  Groovisions

For
  Groovisions_
  Designers_
  Tokyo, Japan

Info
  Borrowing the "Post-it-Note" form, Groovisions' card is super
  practical; once it's stuck to your phone, you'll never lose it!
  Various note-pad versions feature different Chappie doll
  illustrations. Groovisions' most famous project/product,
  these life-sized dolls are all one-of-a-kind.

Design
Code.ch
Reto Gehrig_
Ryo Kawaguchi

For
Mach Architektur
GMBH_
Architects_
Zurich, Switzerland

Info
Printed as a sticker, the dense block of red on this card
enables it to be used in a variety of ways, most notably
as a CD security tag.

MACH ARCHITEKTUR GMBH
JAN FISCHER
GEMEINDESTRASSE 26 8032 ZURICH SWITZERLAND
TEL. +41 1 252 84 44 FAX. +41 1 252 84 47
WWW.MACHARCH.CH JAN_FISCHER@MACHARCH.CH
PERSUASIVE PROPORTIONS

MACH ARCHITEKTUR GMBH
DECHEN SHELKAR GERLING
GEMEINDESTRASSE 26 8032 ZURICH SWITZERLAND
TEL. +41 1 252 84 44 FAX. +41 1 252 84 47
WWW.MACHARCH.CH
DECHEN_SHELKAR_GERLING@MACHARCH.CH
PERSISTENT PROPORTIONS

MACH ARCHITEKTUR GMBH
DAVID MARQUARDT
GEMEINDESTRASSE 26 8032 ZURICH SWITZERLAND
TEL. +41 1 252 84 44 FAX. +41 1 252 84 47
WWW.MACHARCH.CH DAVID_MARQUARDT@MACHARCH.CH
PRESTIGIOUS PROPORTIONS

MACH ARCHITEKTUR GMBH
GEMEINDESTRASSE 26 8032 ZURICH SWITZERLAND
TEL. +41 1 252 84 44 FAX. +41 1 252 84 47
WWW.MACHARCH.CH MACH@MACHARCH.CH
POWERFUL PROPORTIONS

A2-GRAPHICS/SW/HK
UNIT G3 35-40 CHARLOTTE ROAD
LONDON EC2A 3PD
T +44 (0)20 7739 4249

A2-GRAPHICS/SW/HK
UNIT G3 35-40 CHARLOTTE ROAD
LONDON EC2A 3PD
T +44 (0)20 7739 4249

A2-GRAPHICS/SW/HK
UNIT G3 35-40 CHARLOTTE ROAD
LONDON EC2A 3PD
T +44 (0)20 7739 4249

Design
A2-Graphics/SW/HK

For
A2-Graphics/SW/HK_
Designers_
London, UK

Info
Using a rubber stamp on coated stock, A2's first, impromptu business card solution produced uniquely atmospheric results.

Design
Fauxpas Grafik
Gilles Bachmann_
Martin Stillhart

For
Fauxpas Grafik_
Designers_
Zurich, Switzerland

Info
A collection of rubber stamps, including mug-shots, fill various
bureaucratic boxes with an ironic reference to Swiss efficiency.

Andrew Diprose

07957 153 112

andrewdiprose@hotmail.com

Andrew Diprose

07957 153 112

andrewdiprose@hotmail.com

Design
  Andrew Diprose

For
  Andrew Diprose_
  Art director_
  London, UK

Info
  Combining hand and machine, Andrew used an instant card
  printing machine "on its most minimal setting", adding hand-
  stamped macho skulls in pretty rainbow inks to create one-offs.

254

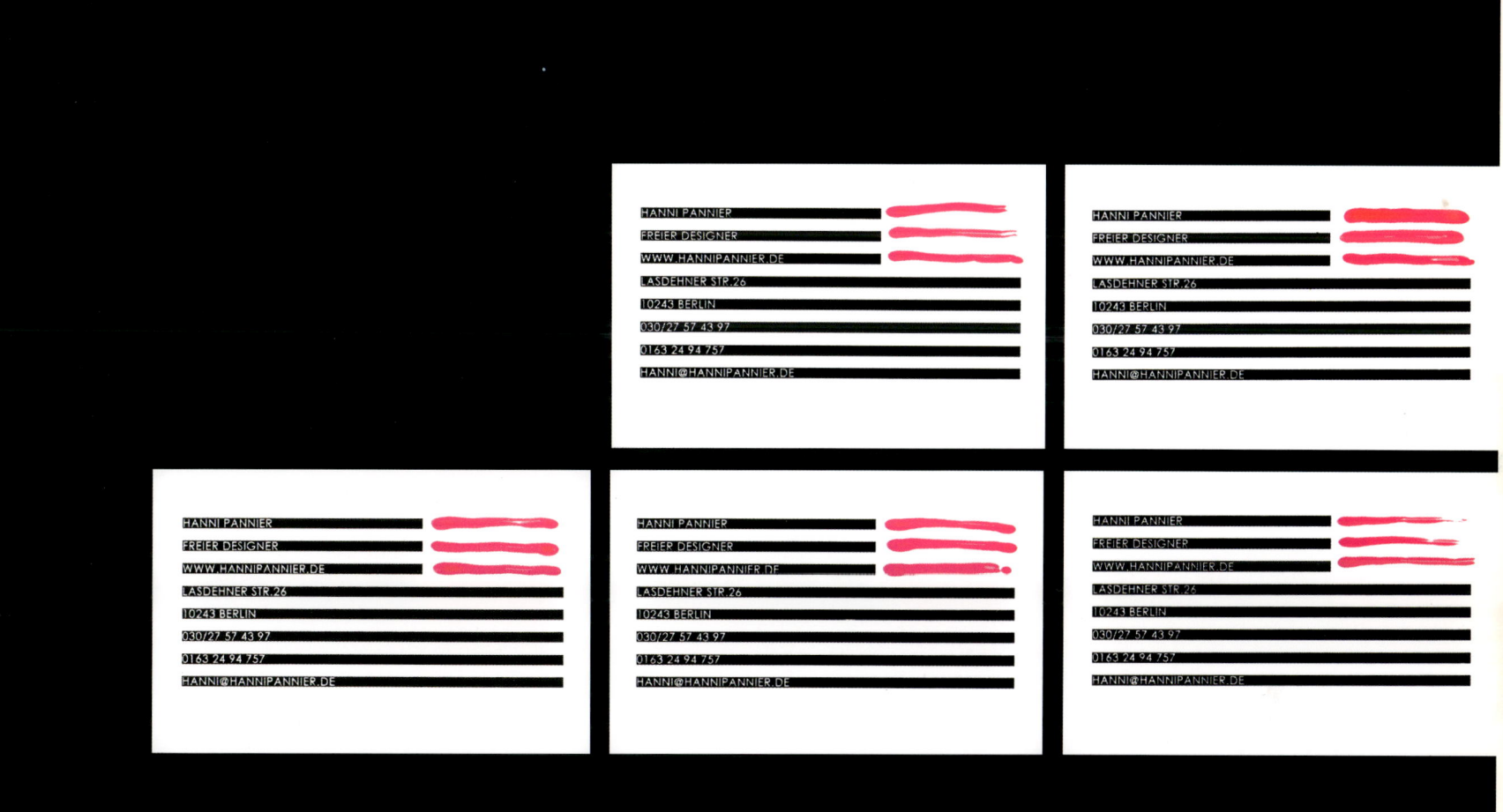

Design
  Hanni Pannier

For
  Hanni Pannier_
  Designer_
  Berlin, Germany

Info
  Each card is completed by hand with an eye-catching pink ink.

Design
Karen Jane

For
Karen Jane_
Designer_
London, UK

Info
Begun as a college project, the recycling of other people's business cards and various found stock, via a distinctive address label, satisfied both Karen's need for plenty of low-cost stationery, and her interest in the history of objects, the past life of these cards, and where they might be diverted to.

draw

scatter

fold

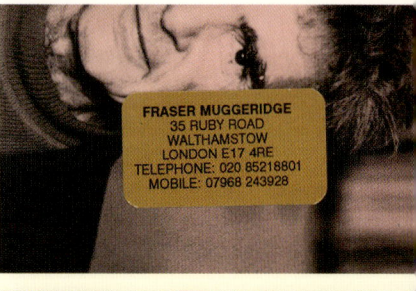

FRASER MUGGERIDGE
35 RUBY ROAD
WALTHAMSTOW
LONDON E17 4RE
TELEPHONE: 020 85218801
MOBILE: 07968 243928

phantoms, vampires, nameless terror, the irrat
unutterable…. It is nostalgia, it is reverie, it is
dreams, it is sweet melancholy and bitter mela
solitude… the sense of a
roaming… ally the East,
remote t le Ages."
Isaiah Be ticism
Isaiah Berlin's words from the Mellon Lectures, a se
of talks on romanticism given at the National Gallery

www.21publishing.com
or general enquiries, email info@21publishing.com
or general sales information, email sales@21publishing.com
or press enquiries, email press@21publishing.com
blishing.com
o join our mailing lis about new
les and events, ema

rade orders
K, Europe and rest of world

ured scorn on some of the other occupations he had followe
owever I don't think he would have reached the rank of
ajor in the army, or held the post of deputy editor of the
ily Telegraph w d considerable
ministrative a work at incredi
eed. Once in t one rang. It wa
e editor of the Could Dad help
ey were short dition. It was
question of finding the newspaper, selecting an item of
erest, and then writing the leader. All this Dad did in a
ort space of time, and soon the article was on its way to the
ht editor's desk. During his long professional life I have

RUTH &

Design
Fraser Muggeridge

For
Fraser Muggeridge_
Designer_
London, UK

Info
One-off cards are cut from recently printed jobs, and with
the addition of a gold-coloured change of address sticker,
each becomes a miniature portfolio-taster. The intrigue
works: the entire item is often requested for inspection.

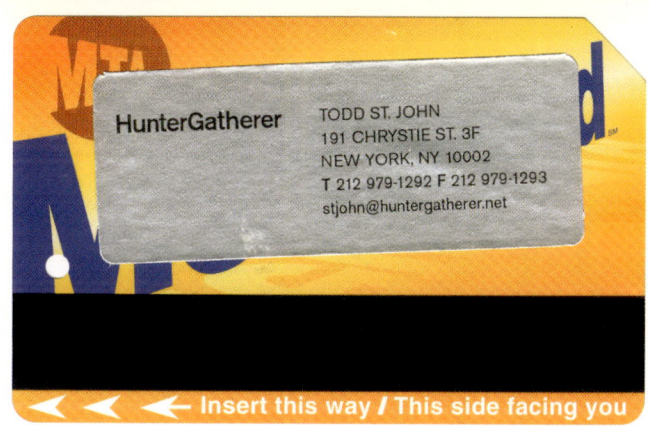

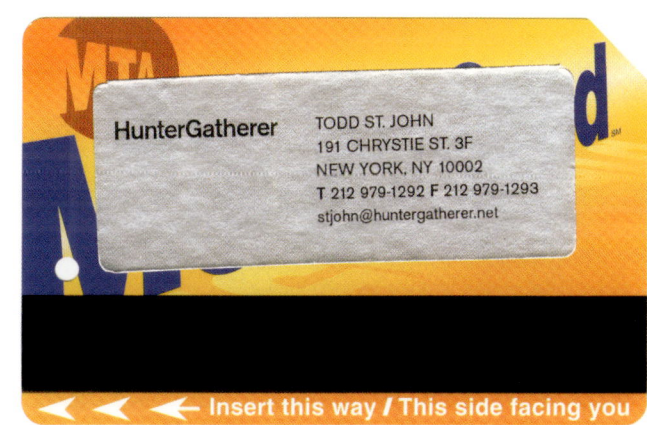

Design
HunterGatherer

For
HunterGatherer_
Clothing label/
designers_
New York, USA

Info
A New York City subway card, with the addition of a sticker,
emphasizes this studio's working method of "collecting, processing,
putting back out".

Design
  Boris Brumnjak

For
  Boris Brumnjak_
  Designer_
  Berlin, Germany

Info
Every other month Boris designs a new limited-edition card; he calls it "the game", and likes to "search for new means to express oneself". As an antidote to commercial projects he seeks out concepts that will inspire people to think again.

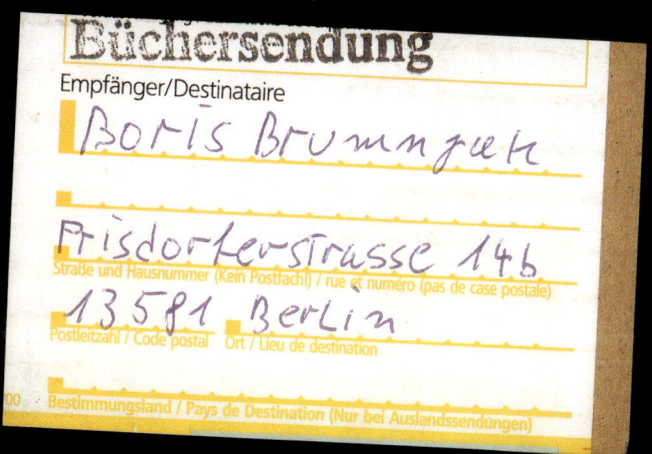

Büchersendung

Empfänger/Destinataire

Boris Brumnjak

Prisdorferstrasse 14b

Straße und Hausnummer (Kein Postfach) / rue et numéro (pas de case postale)

13581 Berlin

Postleitzahl / Code postal   Ort / Lieu de destination

00   Bestimmungsland / Pays de Destination (Nur bei Auslandssendungen)

Abgereist
ohne Adressangabe
Parti
sans laisser d'adresse
Partito
senza lasciare indirizzo

Herr
Boris Brumnjak
Prisdorferstr. 14 B
DE-13581 Berlin

NOM/PRENOM
BRUMNJAK, Boris
ADRESSE
Prisdorferstr. 14 B
13581 Berlin   45
PAYS   TEL:
Germany   030/3663702

Verkehrsunfalldienst

Der Polizeipräsident in Berlin. Moritzstr. 10

Herrn
Boris Brumnjak
Prisdorfer Str. 14 B
13581 Berlin

BORIS BRUMNJAK

PRISDORFERSTR 14B

13581 BERLIN

DE

261

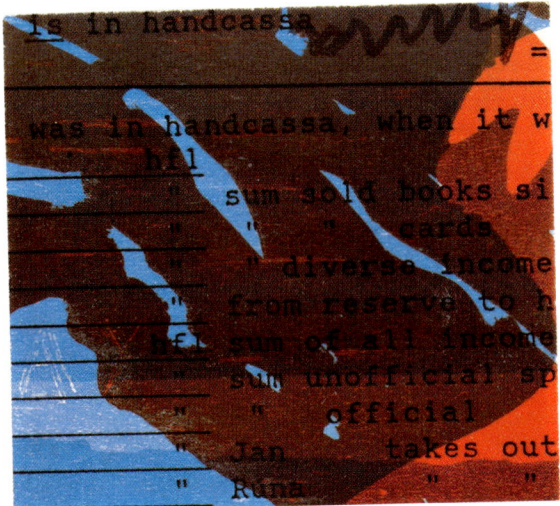

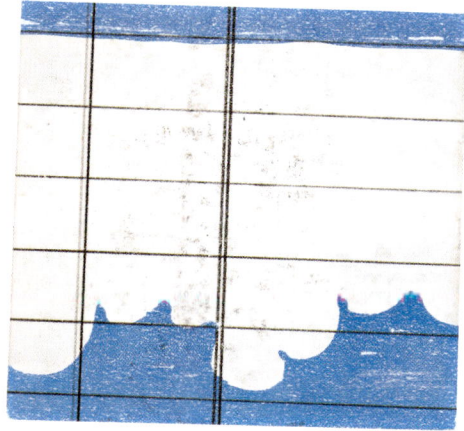

Design
Boekie Woekie

For
Boekie Woekie_
Artists' bookshop_
Amsterdam,
The Netherlands

Info
With address details stamped on cut-up proof pages, these
cards from an artists' bookshop mirror the hand-made
creativity on offer.

Boekie Woekie, books by artists
Berenstraat 16
NL 1016 GH Amsterdam
weekdays 12:00-18:00
T + F +31-(0)20-6390507
e-mail boewoe@xs4all.nl
www.boekiewoekie.com

Boekie Woekie, books by artists
Berenstraat 16
NL 1016 GH Amsterdam
weekdays 12:00-18:00
T + F +31-(0)20-6390507
e-mail boewoe@xs4all.nl
www.boekiewoekie.com

Please send me details

Sam Winston
Designer

42a Peckham Rd
Camberwell
London
SE5 8PX
w_sam@yahoo.com

07970 984414
Artist
Studio 100
100 de Beauvoir Rd
London
N1 4EN
sam@dontpushpress.com

Sam Winston
Designer

42a Peckham Rd
Camberwell
London
SE5 8PX
w_sam@yahoo.com

07970 984414   Sam Winston
Artist   Designer
Studio 100
100 de Beauvoir Rd
London
N1 4EN
sam@dontpushpress.com

Design
  Sam Winston

For
  Sam Winston_
  Designer_
  London, UK

Info
This artist/designer carries his business card – a rubber stamp –
with him, grabbing any scrap of paper at the end of a meeting
for a quick conversion. At other times cards are carefully tailored
to the recipient, via appropriated texts from printed matter.

29 30 31 32 33 34 35 36 37 38 39 40

07970 984414 Sam Winston
Artist Designer
Studio 100
100 de Beauvoir Rd
London
N1 4EN
sam@dontpushpress.com

42a Peckham Rd
Camberwell
London
SE5 8PX

:A Agfa PHOTO

3 black

1 red

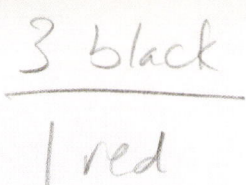
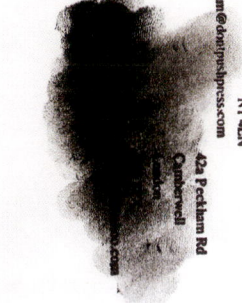

07970 984414 Sam Winston
Artist Designer
Studio 100
100 de Beauvoir Rd
London
N1 4EN
sam@dontpushpress.com

42a Peckham Rd
Camberwell
London
SE5 8PX

Design/illustration
Mysterious Al

For
Mysterious Al_
Designer/illustrator_
London, UK

Info
Drawing and collaging his baggy-eyed characters on to
any card stock, while sometimes morphing the shape,
illustrator and all-round dogsbody Mysterious Al represents
his world view in miniature.

Design
 PMH Master
 Tim Head

For
 PMH Master_
 Designer/illustrator_
 London, UK

Info
 Forget standard formats, PMH is the master of found imagery,
 appropriating all kinds of print material (including calling cards
 of another sort). He adds signature "black letter" type, graf-writing
 and pen and correction fluid patterning to the mix.